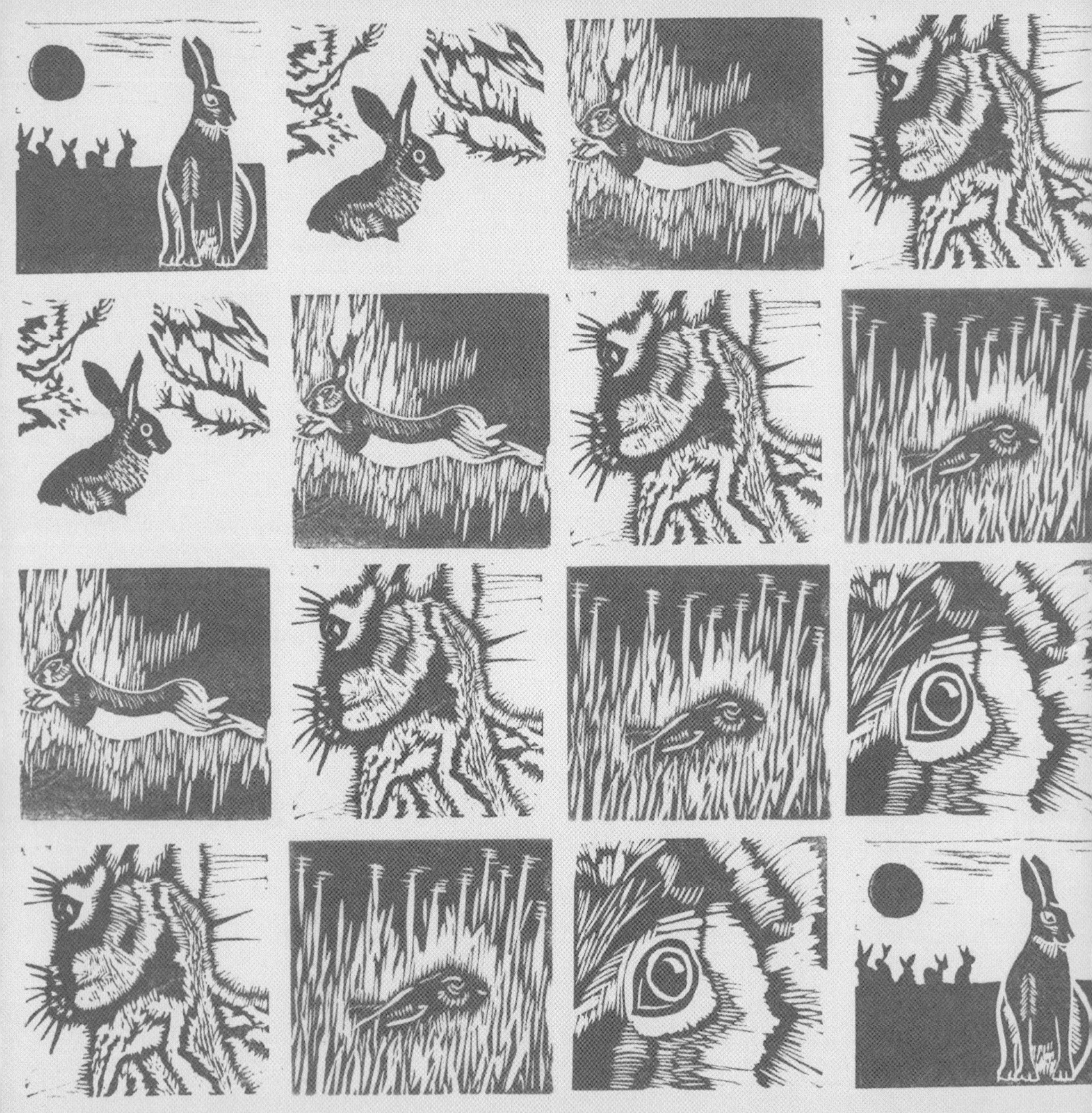

The Hare Book

Edited by Jane Russ
The Hare Preservation Trust

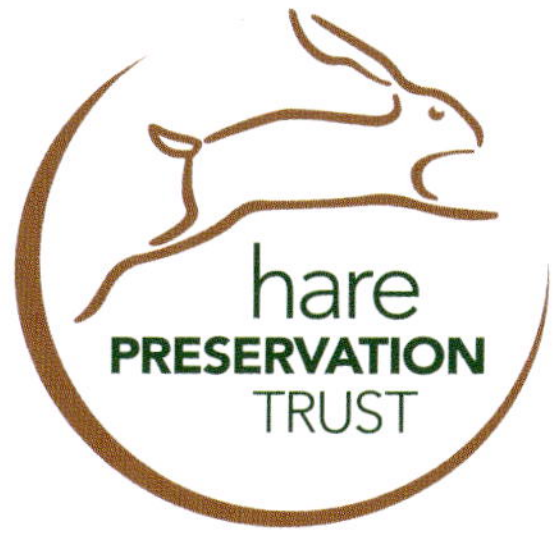

GRAFFEG

Dedications

To the memory of HPT member
Deborah Peers, (1970-2014) whose
generosity has enabled the HPT to
fund this project. Deborah loved
hares and this book will be a lasting
reminder of why.

Contents

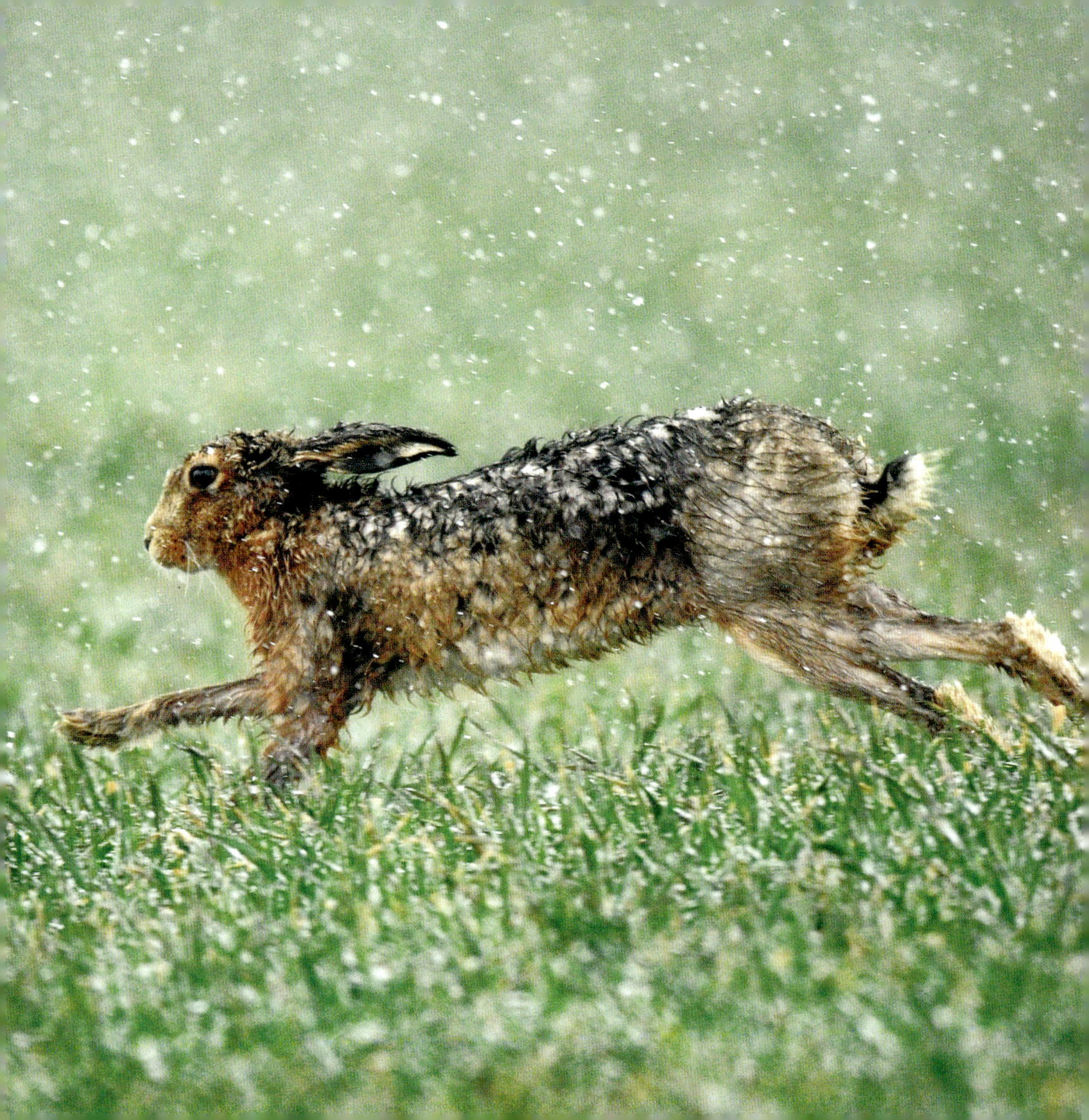

Why a hare is not a rabbit

There are anatomical differences between rabbits and hares; most obvious are the longer ears and back legs of the hare and, not so obvious, the larger size of its heart and volume of circulating blood which enable it to run at speeds of up to 45 miles per hour – that's faster than a puma and much faster than a rabbit! Unlike rabbits, a hare's top lip is split right up to its nose. Sometimes old hares' teeth will protrude through this gap.

There are four simple and easily remembered differences between rabbits and hares:

i) hares shelter in a hollow depression above ground known as a form, rabbits live in burrows underground.

ii) hares are born fully furred, rabbits are born bald.

iii) hares are born with their eyes open, rabbits with their eyes shut.

iv) hares' eyes have a distinctive orange iris, rabbits' eyes have a dark brown iris and appear almost black.

Hares belong to a group of animals known as the order *Lagomorpha.* This includes hares, rabbits and their short-eared cousins the pikas, which are found across the Northern Hemisphere. Lagomorphs have changed little since prehistoric times unlike rodents which have evolved in size and shape from the tiny pygmy jerboa to the capybara! Confusingly, the common names of some hares and rabbits are wrongly attributed; for example, American jackrabbits are technically hares whilst Belgian hares are actually a fancy breed of domestic rabbit!

The Chinese name for 'hare' is also sometimes translated as 'rabbit'.

There are three types of hare in Great Britain and Ireland:

Brown or European hare – *Lepus europaeus*

Blue or mountain hare – *Lepus timidus*

Irish hare – *Lepus timidus hibernicus.*

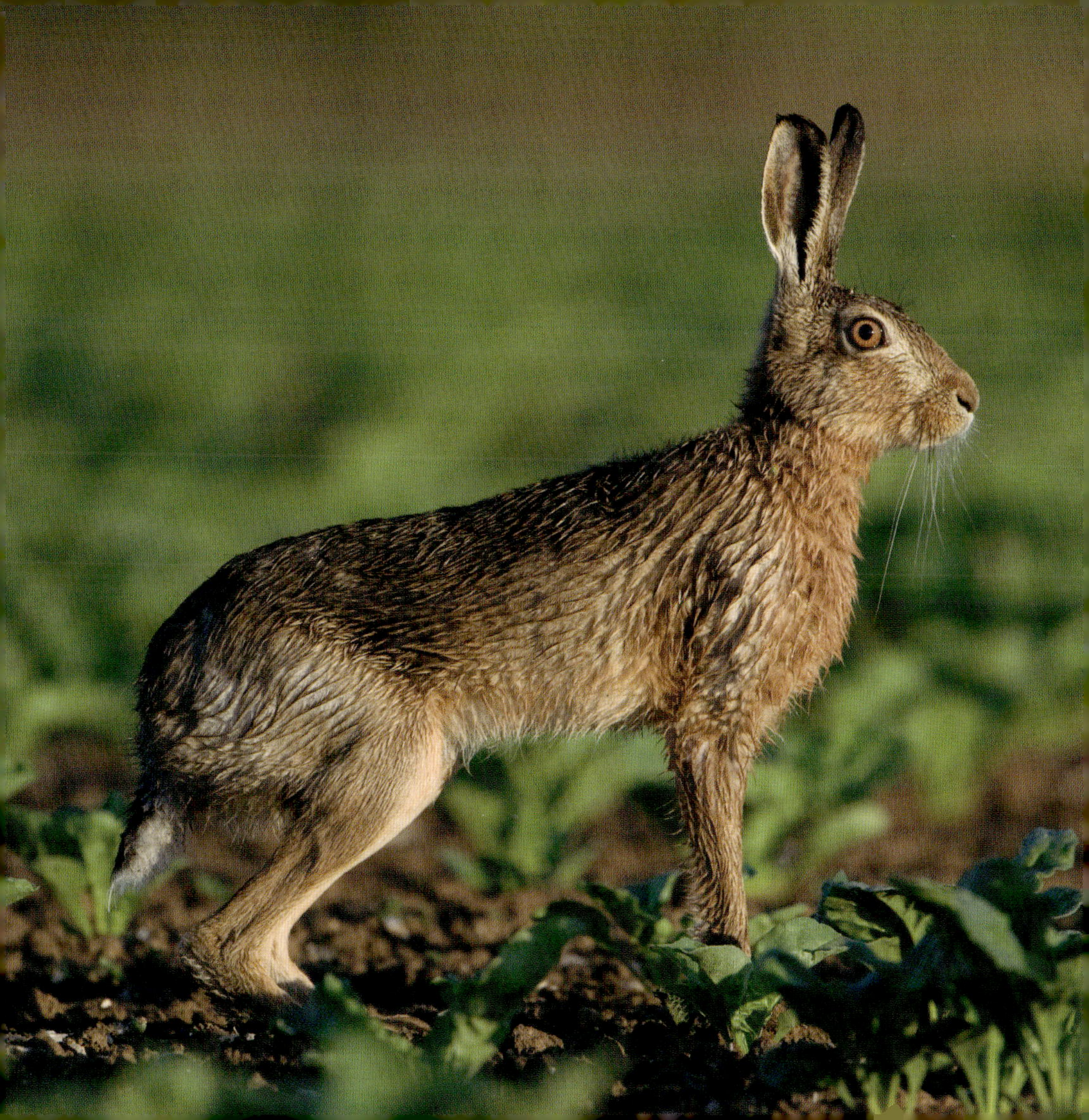

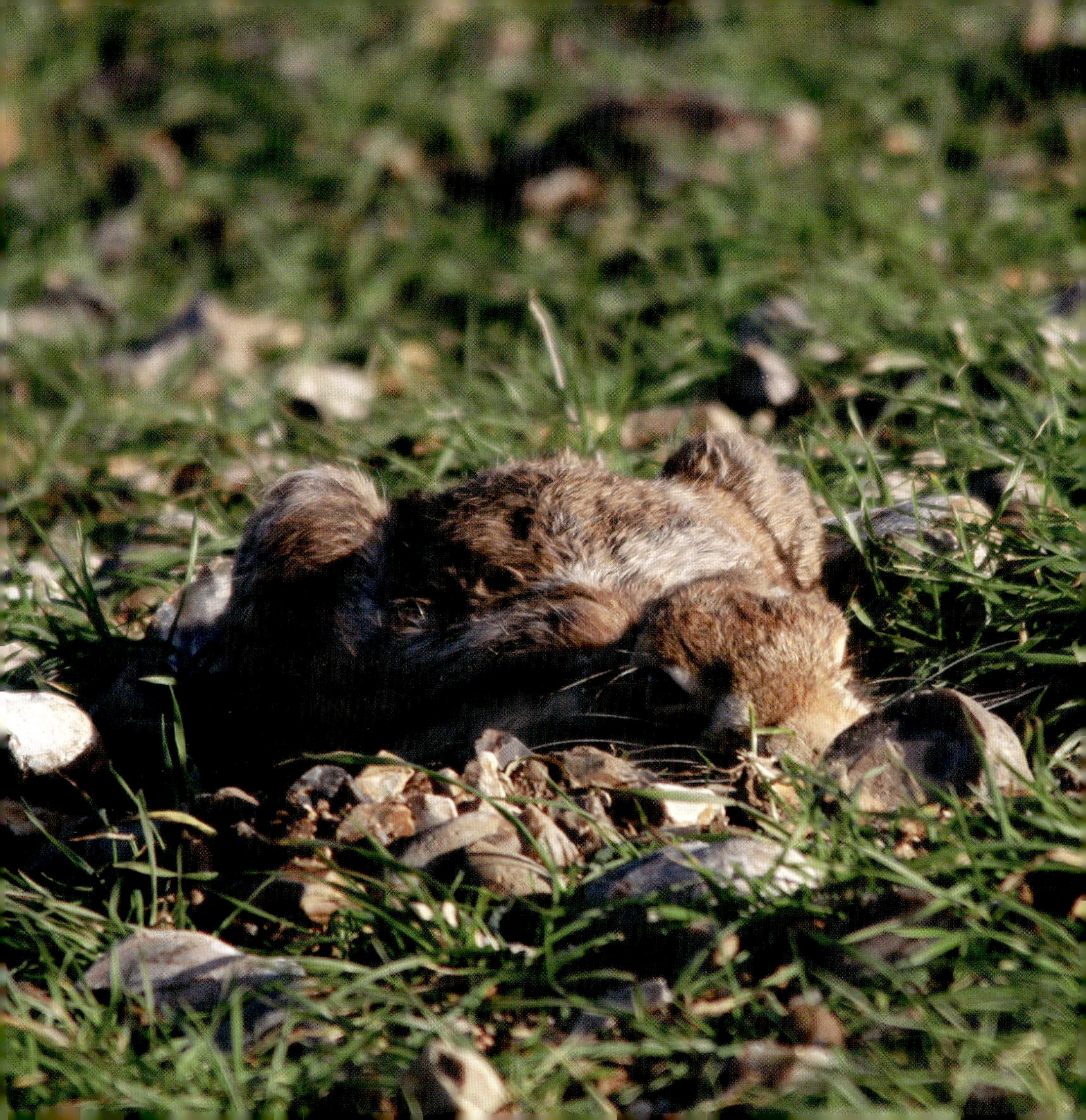

The hare in nature

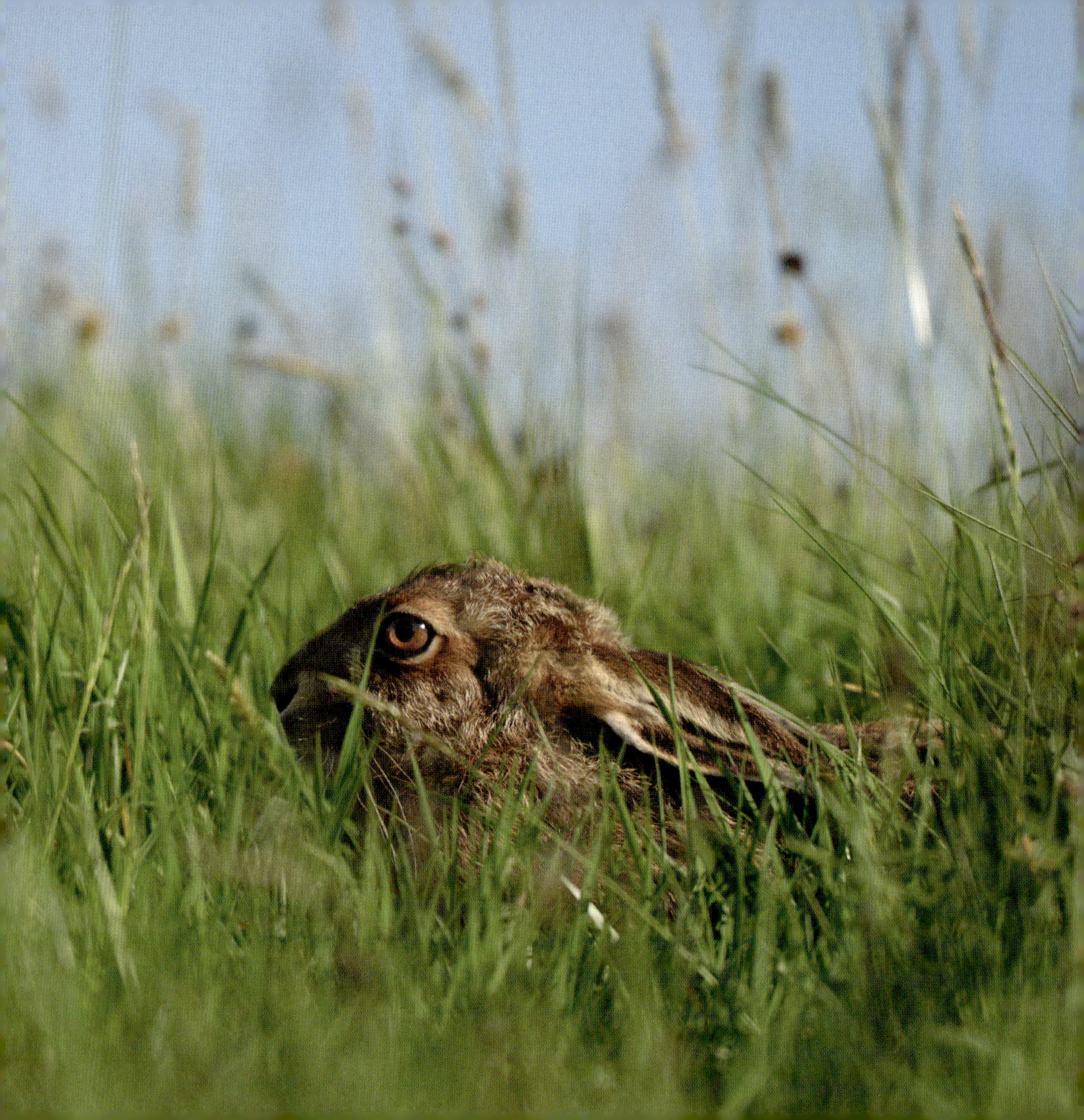

The brown or European hare
Lepus europaeus

It is believed that the brown hare spread into northern Europe after the British Isles were separated from mainland Europe. They are creatures of steppes and plains and evolved in northern Asia after the last Ice Age and spread west as the ice melted. However, there are no actual records of brown hares in the British Isles before the Romans came. Over time, agricultural methods favoured the brown hare and gradually pushed the native mountain hare north into Scotland which remains its UK stronghold. Brown hares are present in some areas of Ireland, but these are believed to have been deliberately introduced around two hundred years ago; the Irish hare is now considered to be a separate species.

Brown hares are the most common species of hare in England; they are also one of the largest and are much bigger than their mountain and Irish hare cousins. Hares do not live in burrows underground but create hollow depressions in the grass or soil in which to shelter; these are known as 'forms'. They will also use man-made 'depressions', such as plough furrows, where they will hunker down low and virtually disappear from sight.

Adults will move around and graze most days unless the weather is very wet when they will sit tight. They are mainly active at night and for this reason are most often seen at dawn and dusk.

Hares can breed all year round if conditions are favourable, however, the main season runs from February to September. The boxing behaviour we associate with spring is most clearly seen at that time of year as crops are low and sight lines are good. Would-be hare suitors are seeking acceptance from the females who will box them away until they are ready to mate. The large hare seen in these competitions is the female, who may be surrounded by a group of males all nipping in to try their luck.

The onset of the breeding season is governed by day length and gestation is normally 40 – 45 days. Hares occasionally become pregnant with a second litter before the first litter is born in a process known as superfoetation. This occurs when a doe is mated and new eggs are fertilized whilst she is already pregnant. This may explain why hares have been seen as fertility symbols. The phenomenon of superfoetation in mammals was speculated upon as far back as the fourth century BC by Aristotle and occurs in other species.

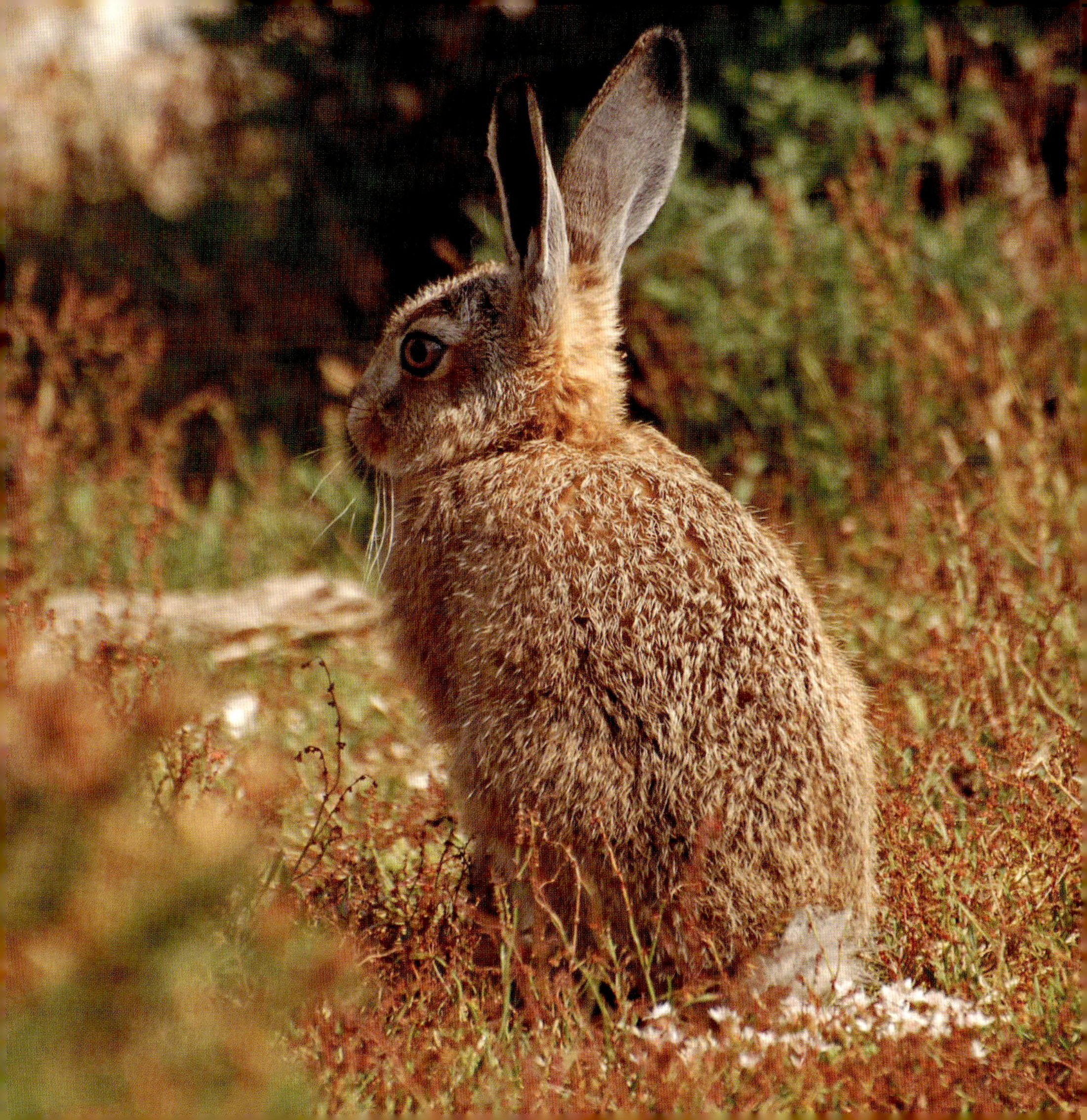

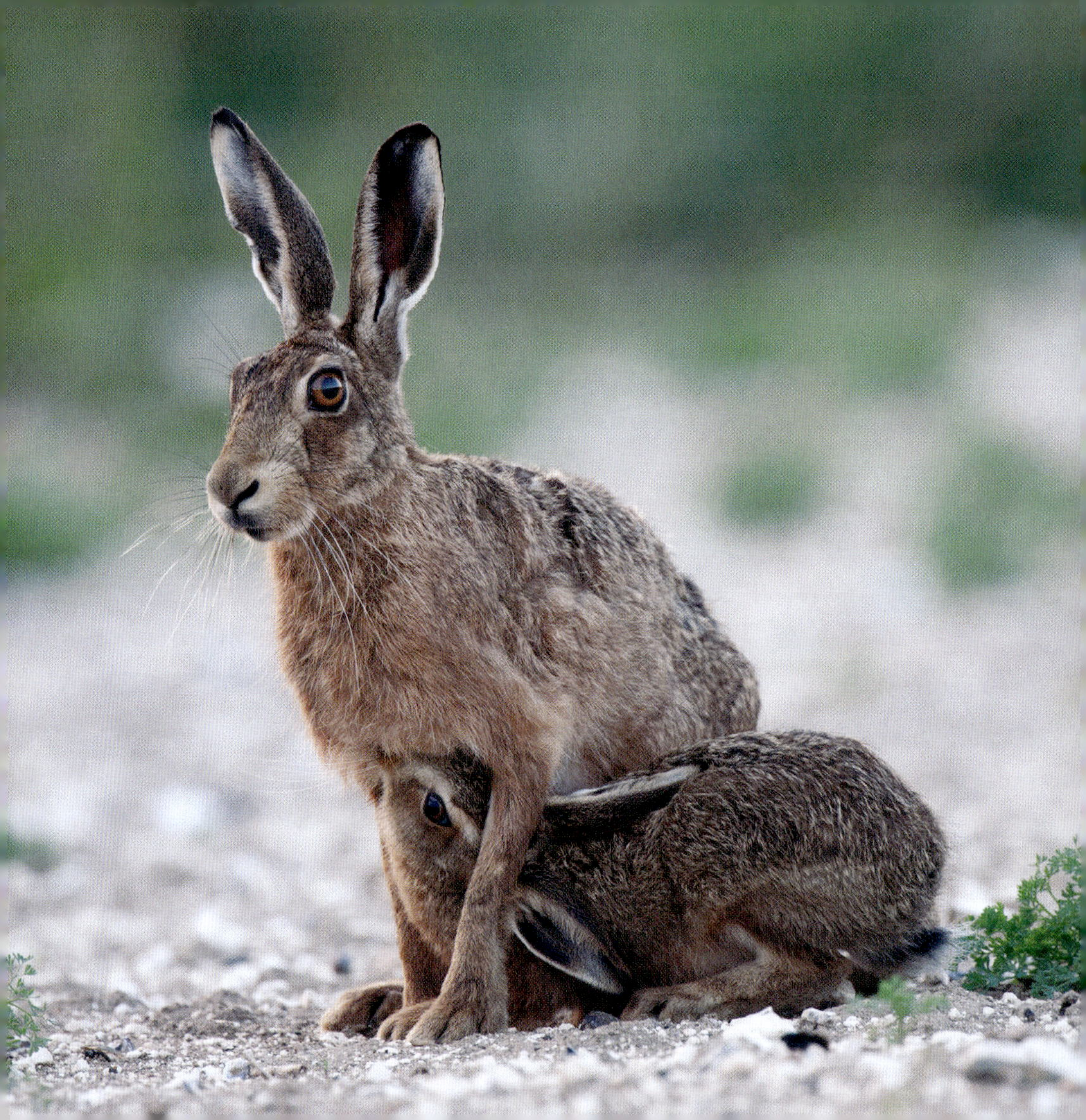

The young of hares, known as leverets, weigh about 100 grams at birth and are weaned after approximately 28 days, suckling can, however, last longer at the end of the season. Litter sizes vary according to how mild the weather is and the age of the mother. The female, jill or doe, can conceive in the calendar year of her own birth but the majority of young female hares first become reproductively active in the spring of the year after their birth, when they reach a weight of about 1.5 kg. They can have up to four litters a year but three is normal.

The doe creates a shallow scrape, or form, in which to give birth, often in long grass or under overhanging vegetation. In contrast to rabbits, which are born blind and bald into a subterranean fur-lined nest, leverets are born fully furred and with their eyes open. The youngsters soon disperse in case they are discovered by a predator – if they are found together, then the whole litter may be lost. The mother will visit once a day to suckle them, usually just after dusk; this only takes a few minutes as hare milk is very rich. As they grow older, the doe will call them to her by 'mewing'; they will leave their forms, suckle and then return to where their mother left them. Observations show that the young hares will stay around the area where they were born, exploring their surroundings, for around four months.

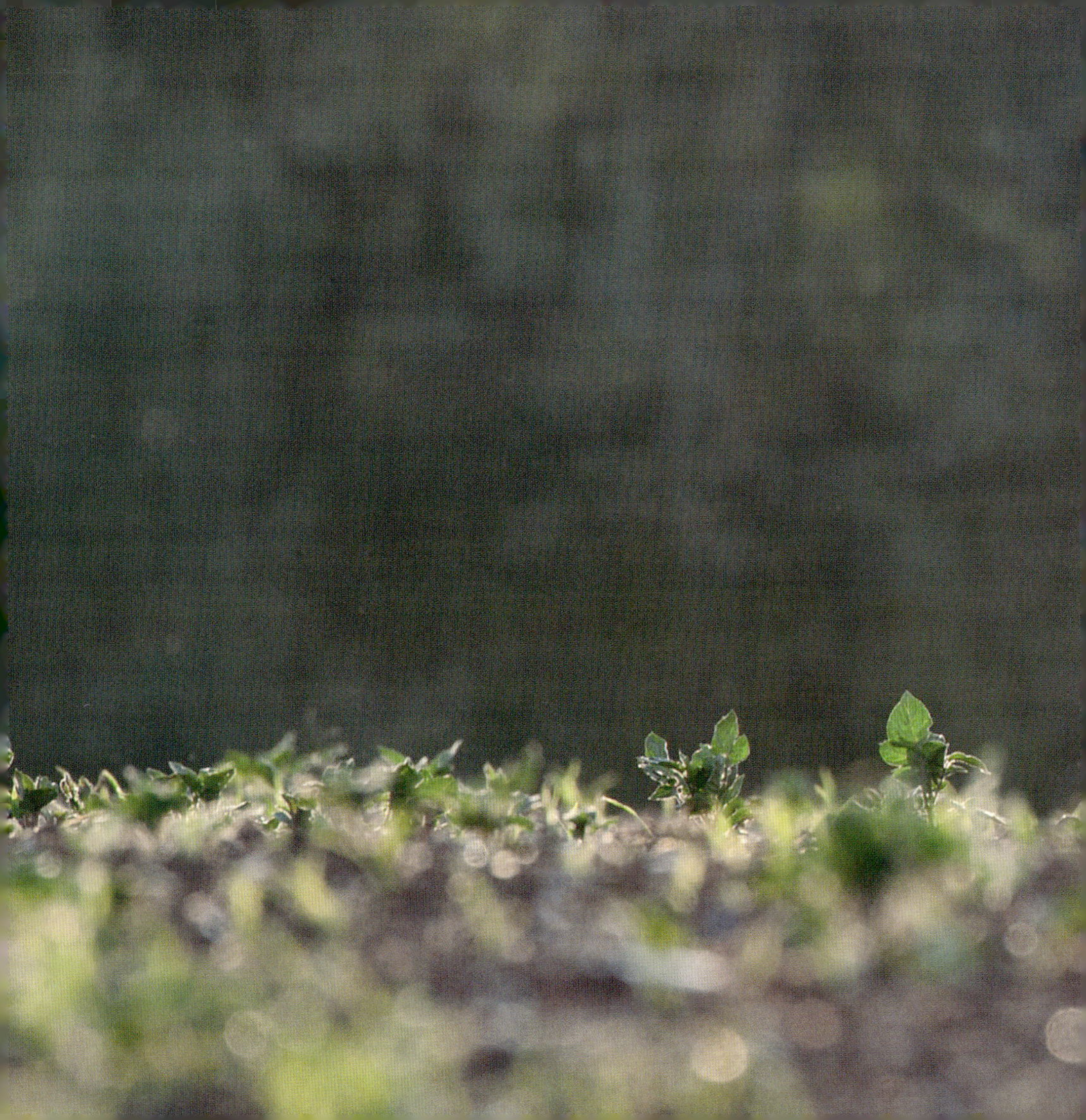

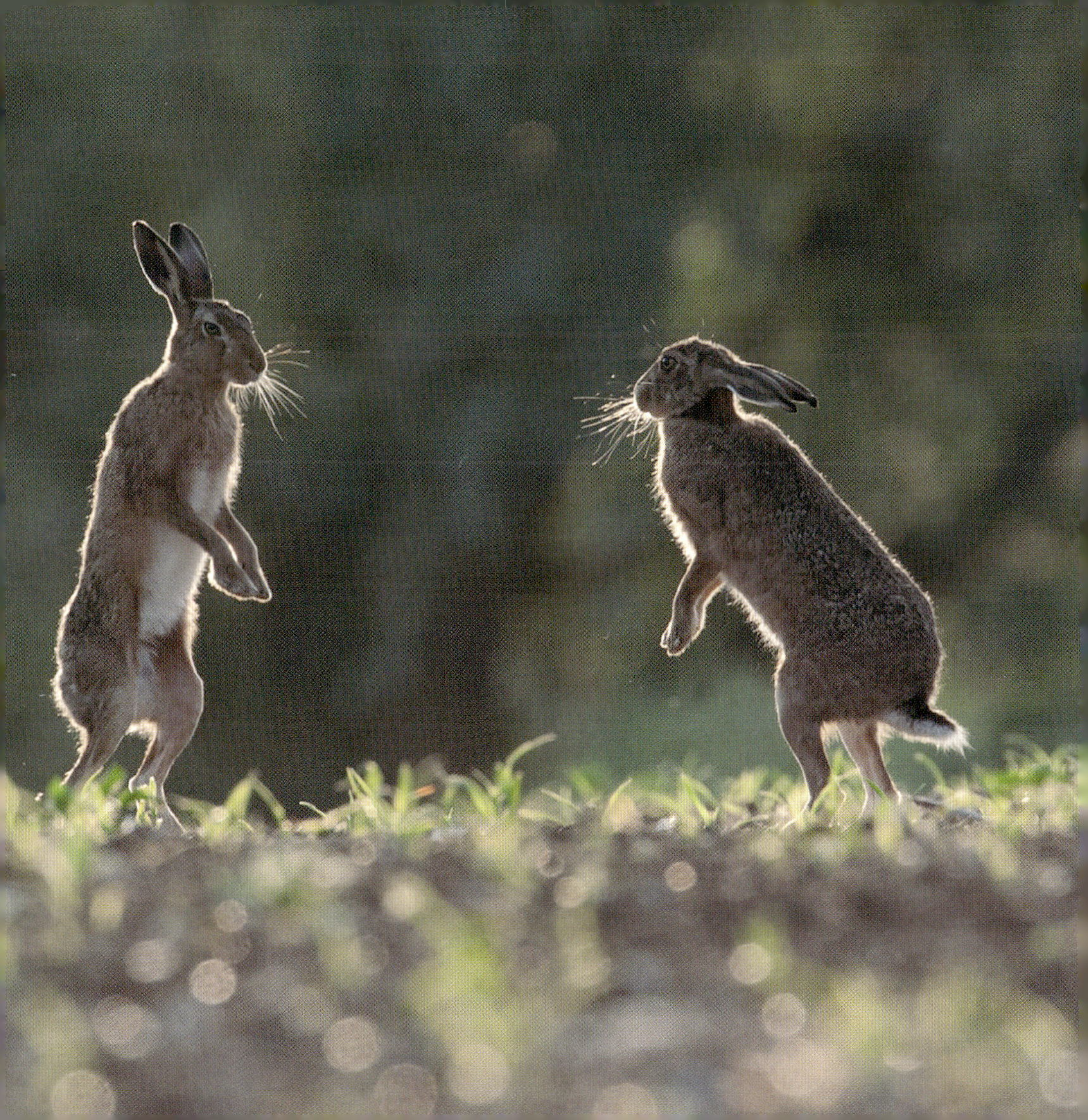

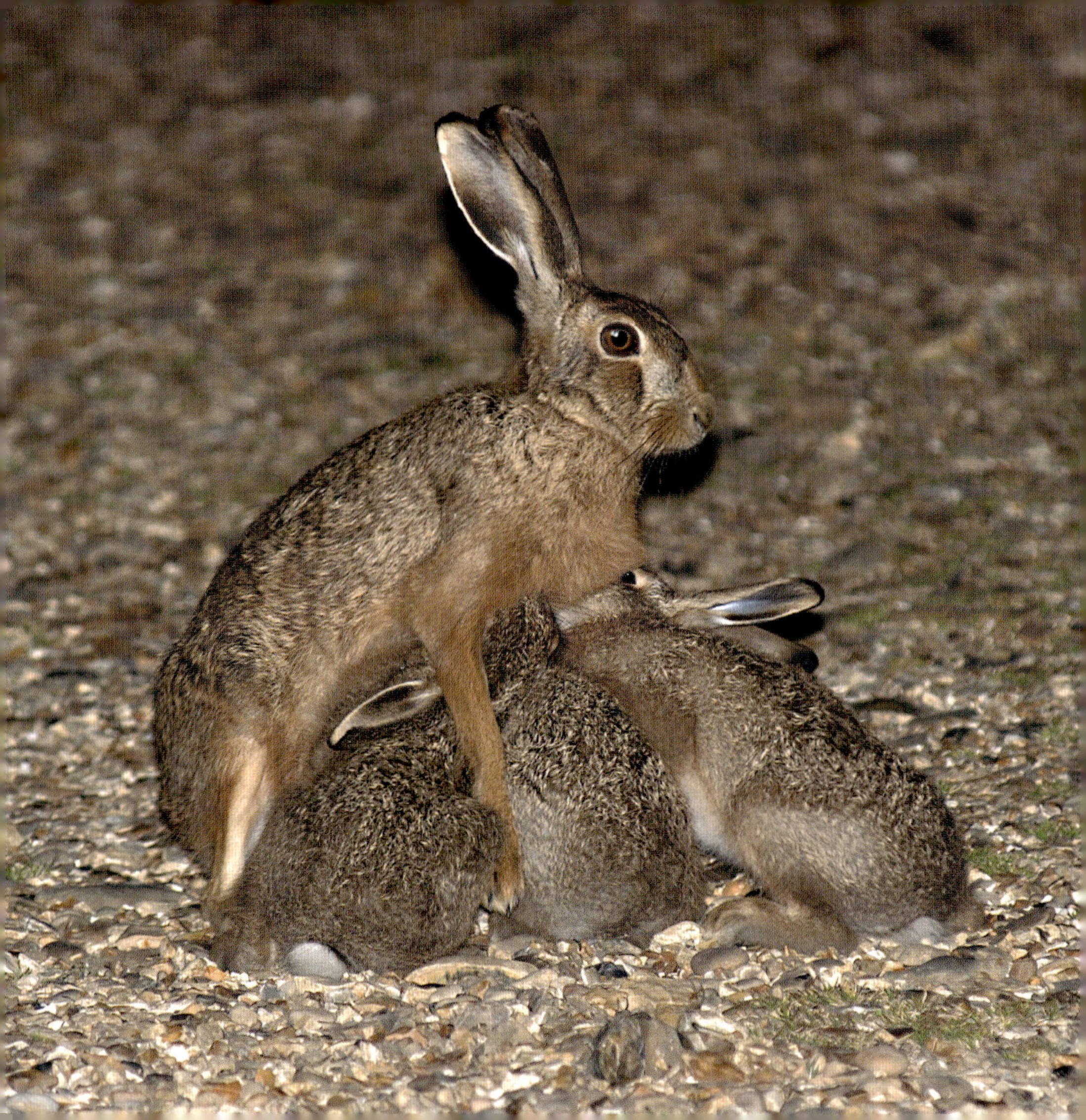

Hare encounter

'The mother came to visit her young in the afternoon long before the feed, as they started to wake in their day scrapes and move about (3.00 pm onwards, but mostly active after 6.00 pm). We had quite a bit of leveret play: jumping in the air, rushing about and twitting passing pheasant and chickens. The mother hung out with her nippers on several occasions, having a sand bath in a flower bed and generally keeping a benevolent eye on them.

There is a strange transition between this informal play and a formal, almost ritual, prelude to the feed itself. With about 20 minutes to go the leverets moved to their pre-feed positions and sat very still. These were the same positions on several nights running, although they varied a little on the last couple of nights before weaning: one sat on a particular paving stone by our back door, another by the back wheel of my Lesley's car, another by a particular daffodil. Each spot was about six to ten feet from the central feeding position on our drive. Then, more or less exactly an hour after sunset, the young rushed together and huddled in a group. They were quickly joined by the mother for the feed, which lasted between a couple of minutes and a few seconds at the end. Then, in a bomb burst of fur the mum and young scampered off, sometimes in different directions, and once all together.

This observation may cast light on the question of whether the mother summons the young to feed with a call of some sort. We didn't hear or see anything and it's just a thought that it's the opposite: it's the visual cue of the leverets huddling together in a tight group that brings the watching mother forward. By way of confirmation of this, the night they were weaned the young still grouped hopefully for their feed even though mum never showed.

The night before they were weaned mum turned up with another hare, presumably her new man. He kept trying to lead her away into the fields, but then she'd return to be with the young and eventually feed them, albeit late; it was clear she had other things on her mind and was quickly away.

On the day they were weaned, Lesley saw the mother arrive a bit earlier than usual and follow the young around. They were dismissive of her attentions, like teenagers of an over-attentive and 'kissy' relative. She did a lot of sniffing of where they'd been sitting; this is conjecture, but maybe she was scenting their urine etc. to see if they had successfully moved to an adult diet, and therefore were safe to leave to fend for themselves. She certainly didn't show for a feed later that night. The mum doesn't abandon the young altogether.

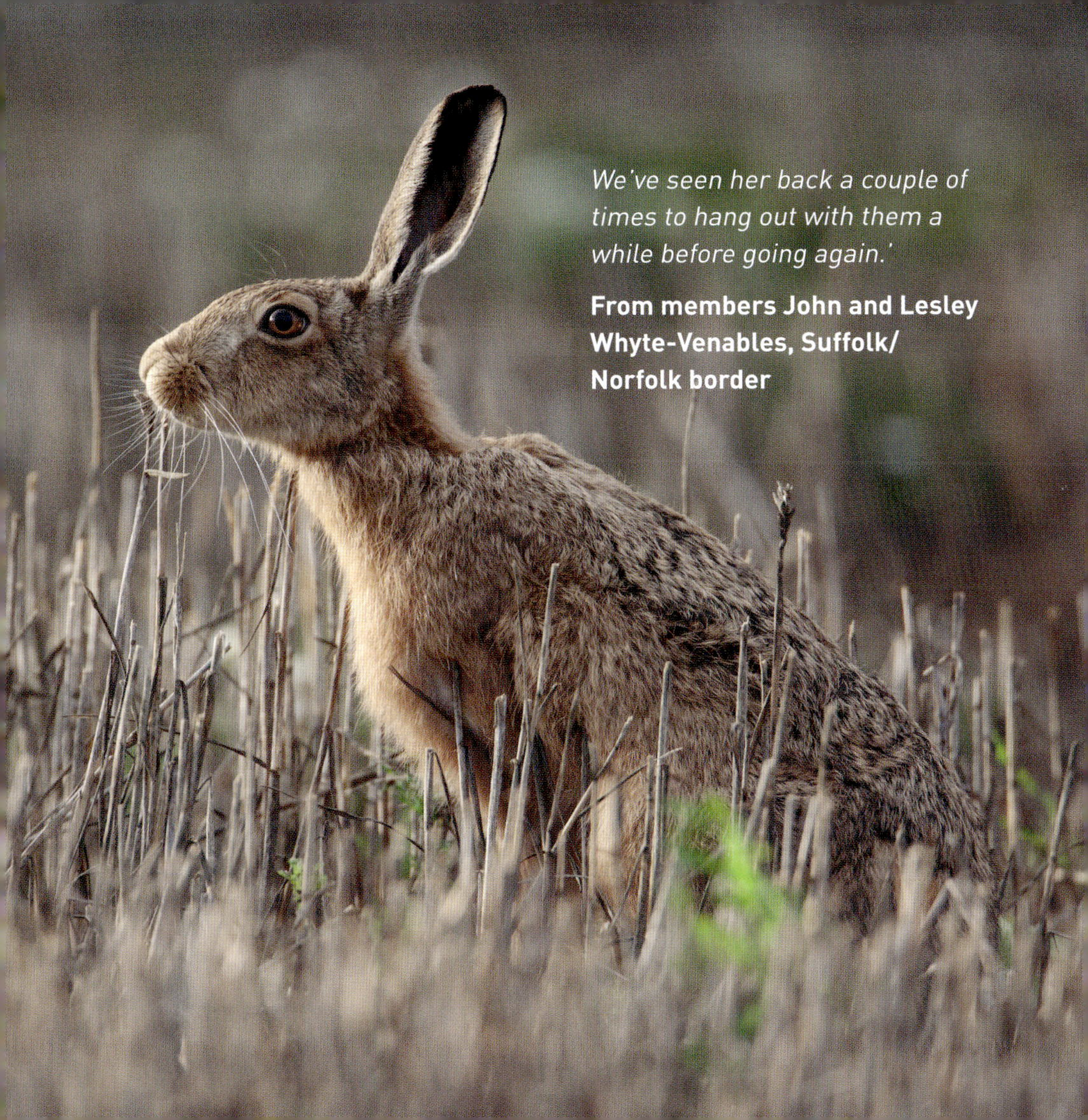
We've seen her back a couple of times to hang out with them a while before going again.'

From members John and Lesley Whyte-Venables, Suffolk/ Norfolk border

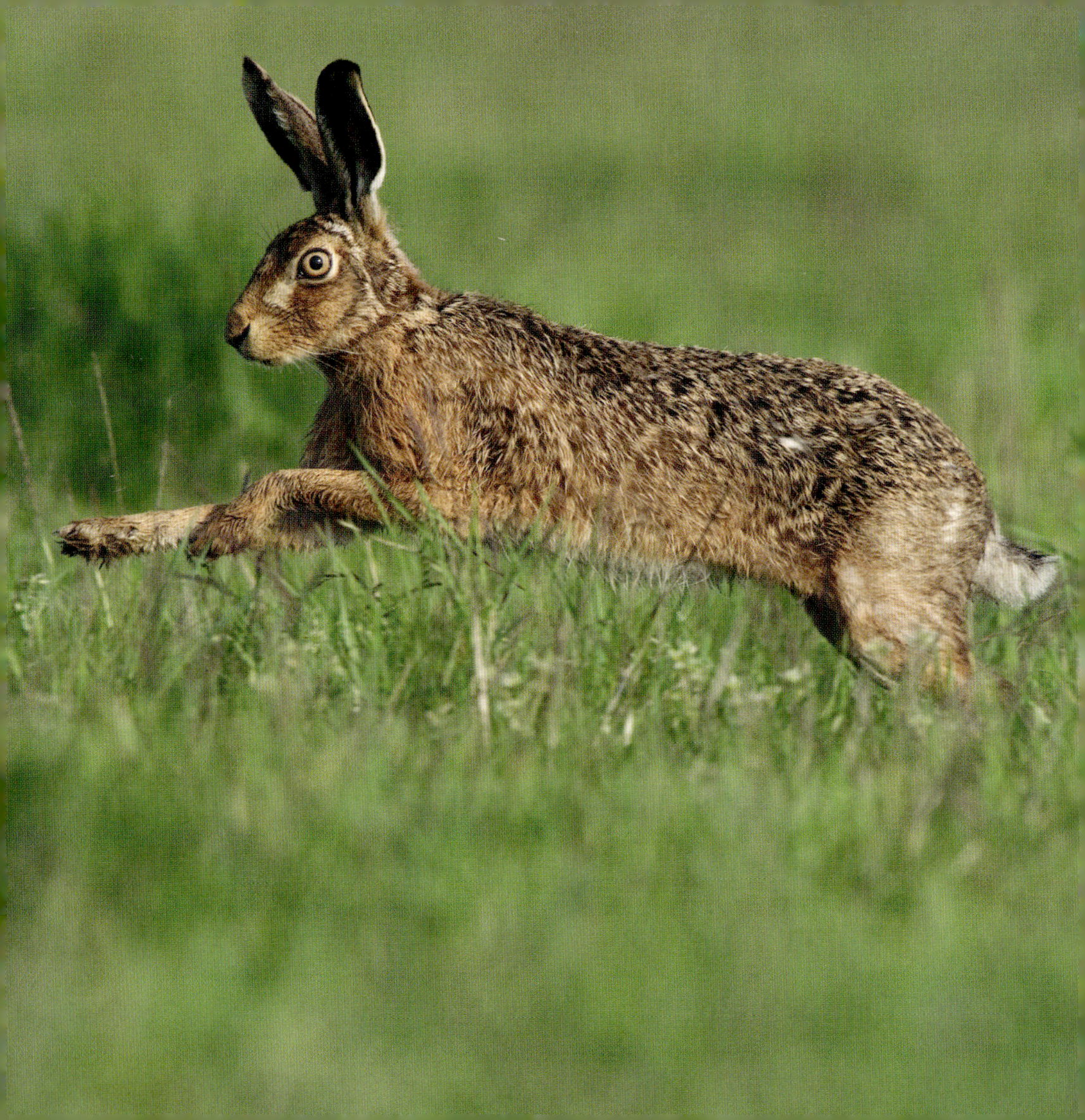

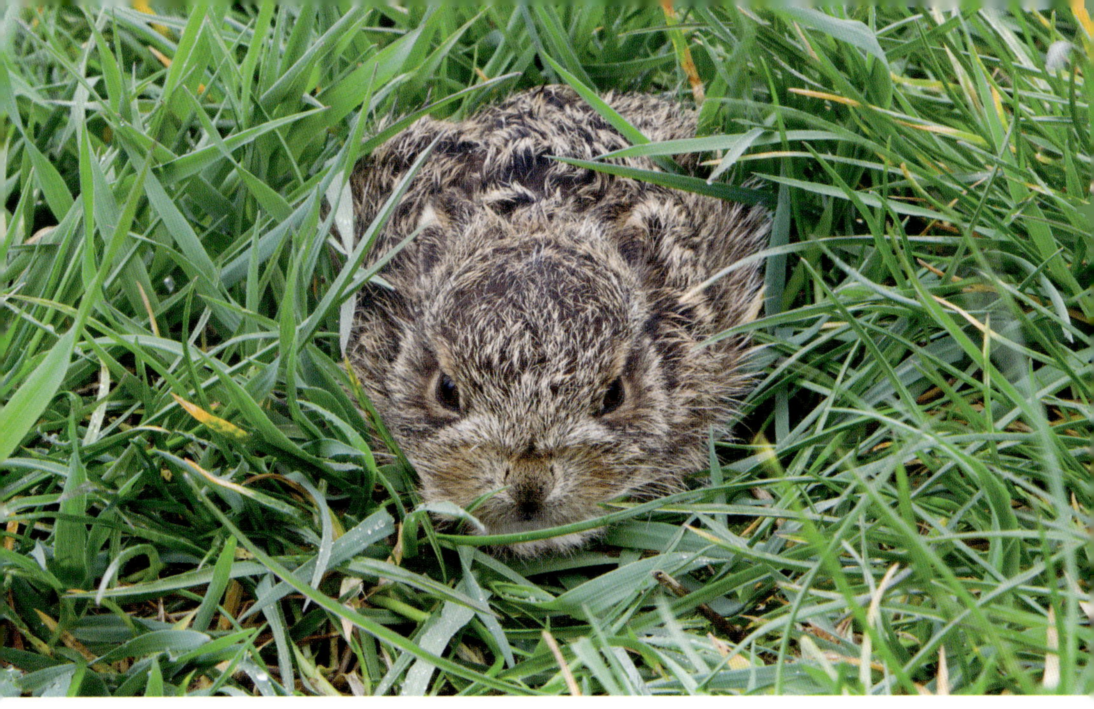

Leverets are occasionally found alone in fields, or indeed in gardens! Although they appear abandoned, it is normal for leverets to be alone for most of the time and their mother will return to feed her offspring around dusk. As with young garden birds, unless they are clearly in immediate danger, leverets should be left undisturbed. If they are in a hazardous situation, or injured, advice should be sought from a professional organisation such as the Hare Preservation Trust.

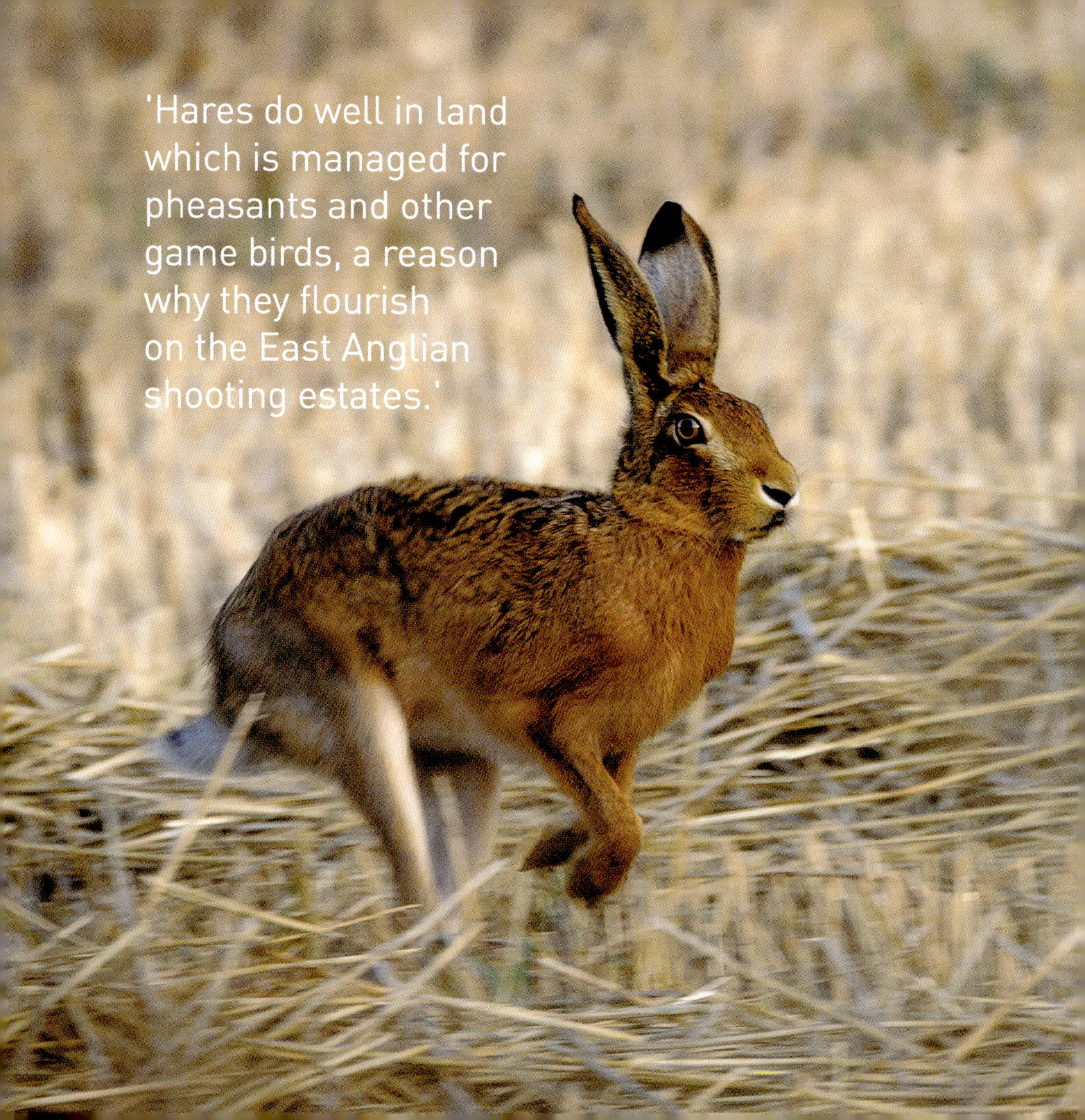
'Hares do well in land
which is managed for
pheasants and other
game birds, a reason
why they flourish
on the East Anglian
shooting estates.'

Tagged hares in Poland have been known to live as long as twelve years and William Cowper recorded in 1787 that one of his pet hares lived to nine years and the other to twelve. In the wild in England it is unlikely a hare will reach more than four years old.

The last serious attempt to assess the national brown hare population was in 1997/98 by Professor Stephen Harris and the Bristol University team, the Mammal Research Group, which indicated that the population had fallen to 730,000 from their previous survey result of 810,000 carried out in 1993/94. There has been no serious independent attempt to organise

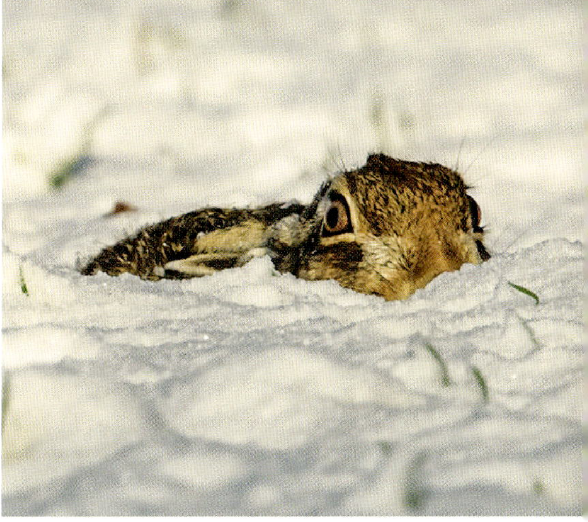

a nationwide assessment of hare numbers since.

Hares do well in land which is managed for pheasants and other game birds, a reason why they flourish on the East Anglian shooting estates. Hare numbers crashed in the late 1960s most probably because of a change in farming practices and also because of the increase in motor traffic.

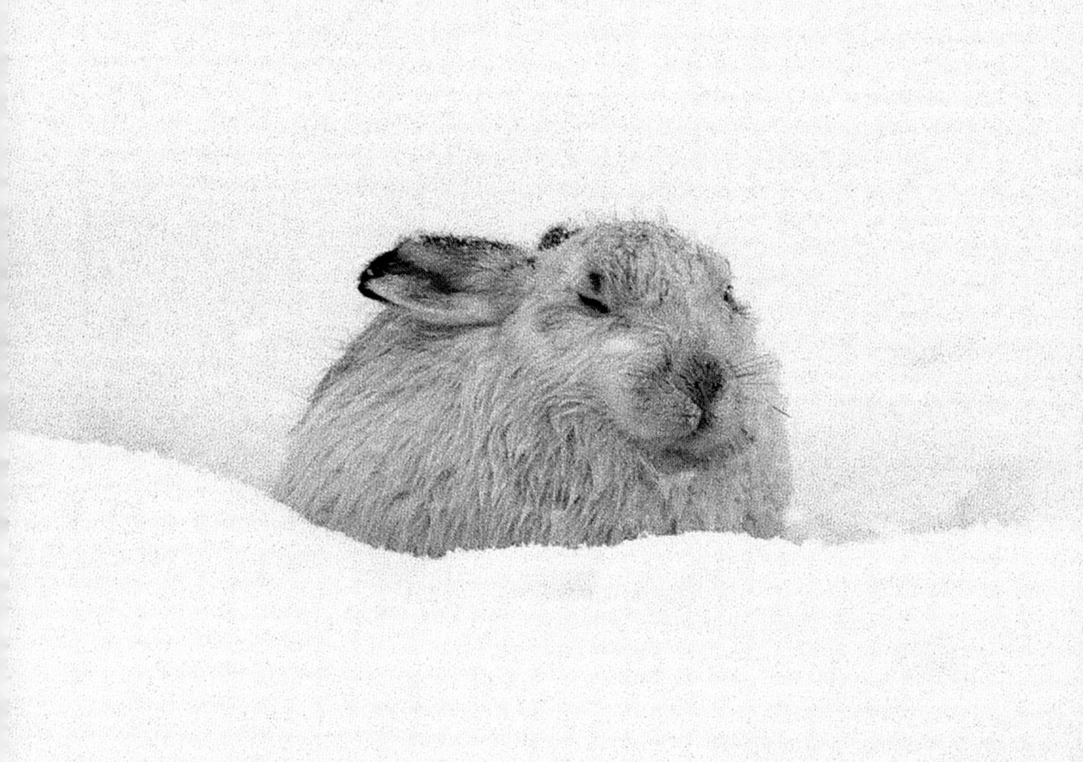

The mountain hare
Lepus timidus (scoticus or alba)

These are the indigenous hares that have been in Britain since the last Ice Age. They have shorter ears than those of the brown hare, and with slightly black tips and a completely white tail. In Britain the mountain hare is associated with heather moorlands, particularly those managed by burning strips for red grouse. It is native to the Highlands of Scotland but the Victorians re-introduced them to the Southern Uplands and the Peak District across to Snowdon: they are also found on some Scottish islands including Hoy (Orkney), Mainland (Shetland), Mull and Skye. They are sometimes considered to be the same species as the Arctic and Greenland hares.

The mountain hares are also known as the blue hare, the white hare, the maukin or, in Gaelic, the *maigheach-gheal*. Research has shown that the mountain hare moults its coat (or pelage) three times a year as opposed to the brown hare's two.

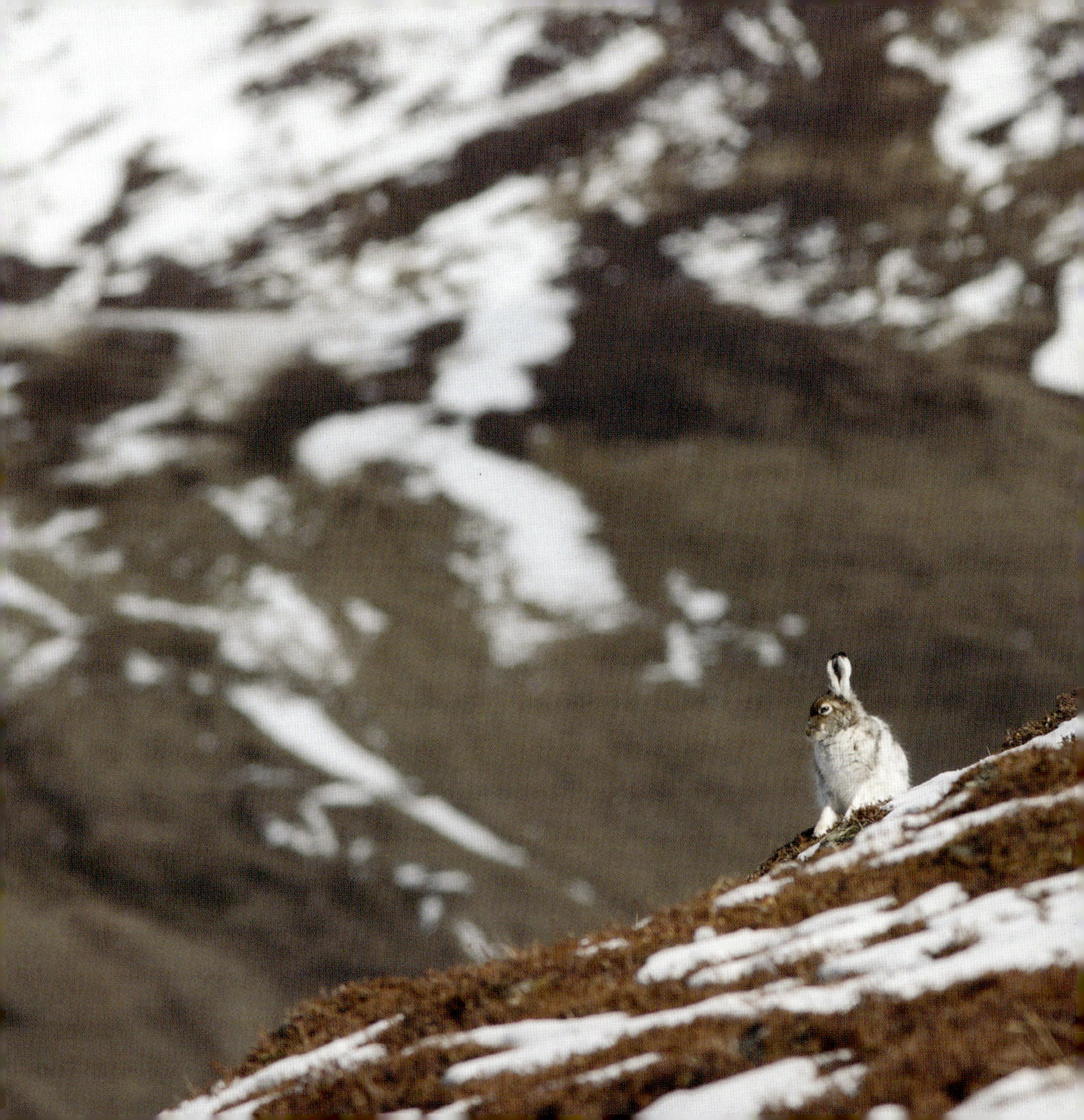

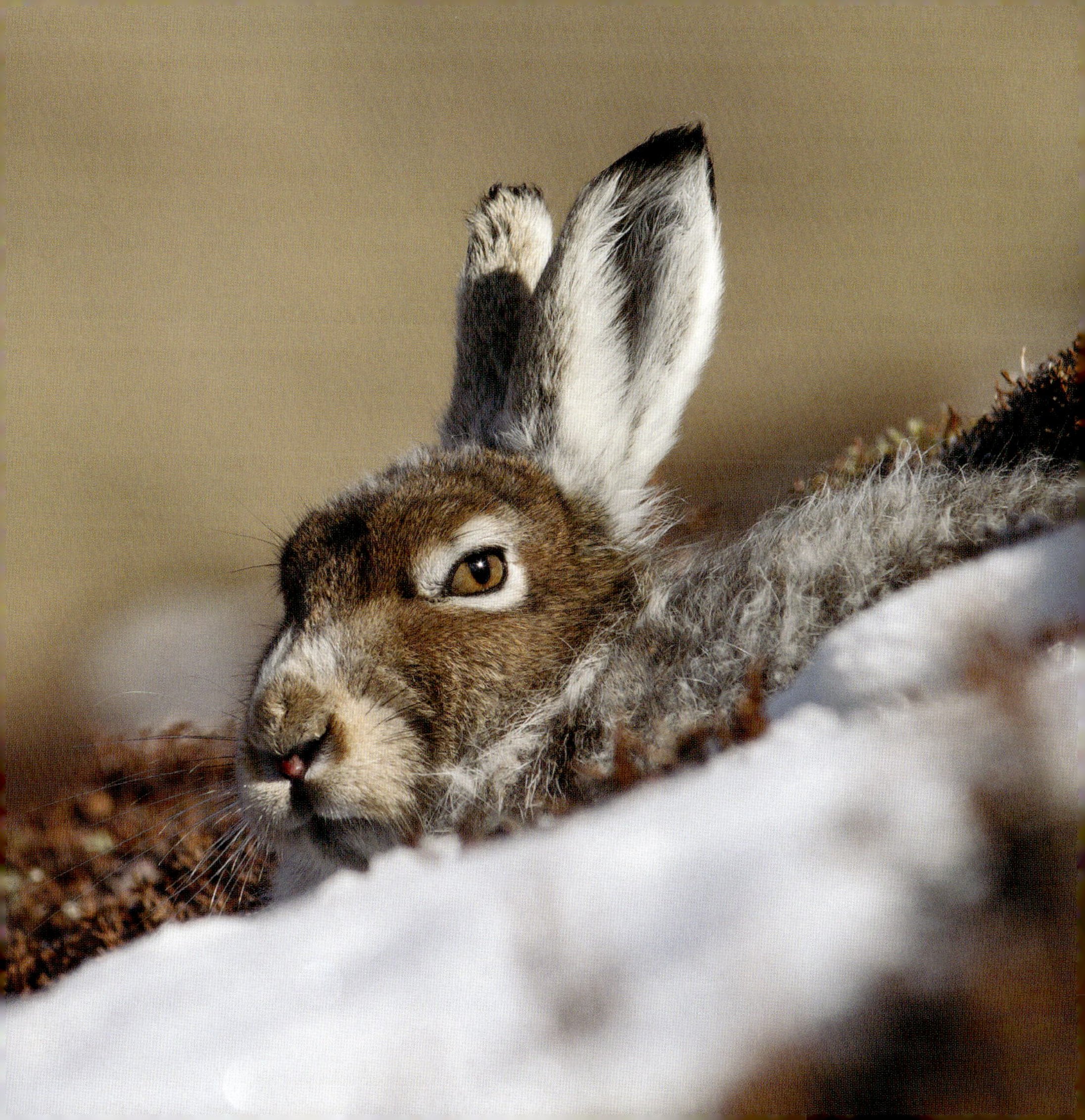

Research has shown that the mountain hare moults its coat (or pelage) three times a year as opposed to the two of the brown hare.

Moult 1: it loses its full white coat in spring and changes to a smoky blueish-brownish one until after midsummer (hence the 'blue hare').

Moult 2: June to August the coat is almost the same colour but with a little hint of white in places.

Moult 3: during the second half of October this coat begins to shed and by December it is back in the full white, longer, thicker fur for overwintering. The tail is white during these changes and the ear tips also remain black throughout.

Due to these colour changes, it has also been known as the variable or varying hare. Very rarely, black mountain hares have been reported.

The moult is dependent upon temperature and appears to be initiated by shortening day lengths so not all individuals necessarily turn completely white. Those at higher altitudes turn white earlier and more completely than those at lower altitudes.

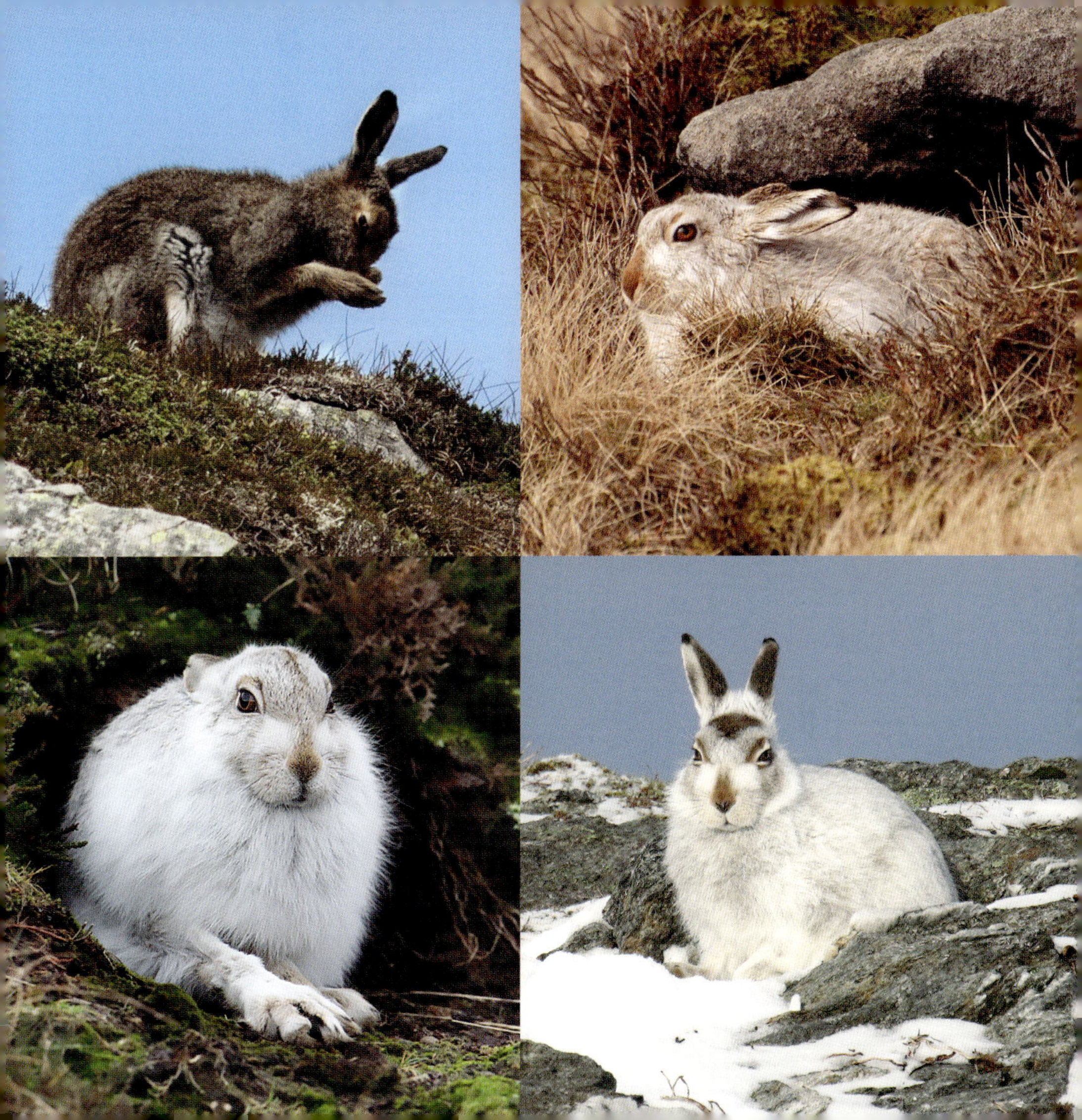

Resting by day in their forms, the mountain hares gather at night to feed in large groups.

Pliny the Elder in 1st century AD says, 'The white hares of the Alps are thought to eat snow in the winter, for they turn colour when the snow melts'. The change of pelage starts at ground level and gradually works its way up to the hare's back until it is mostly white. In the spring the colour change works in reverse, top down, and it is believed that as well as camouflage against the snow from predators like foxes and eagles, the white coat offers some thermal insulation too.

The mountain hare, as you would expect, occupies higher ground than the brown hare, some 350 metres up in the Lammermuirs in the Borders, and 750 to over 1,000 metres in the Cairngorms. The mountain hare's form is deeper than the brown hare's and will be, of necessity, in either snow or soil or under the lea of a heather hummock, with its back to the elements. This sitting with the back to the elements is common to all hares!

Resting by day in their forms, the mountain hares gather at night to feed in large groups. Although considered to be browsers of woody plants such as heather and other dwarf shrubs and trees, they prefer to eat grasses when available during the summer months.

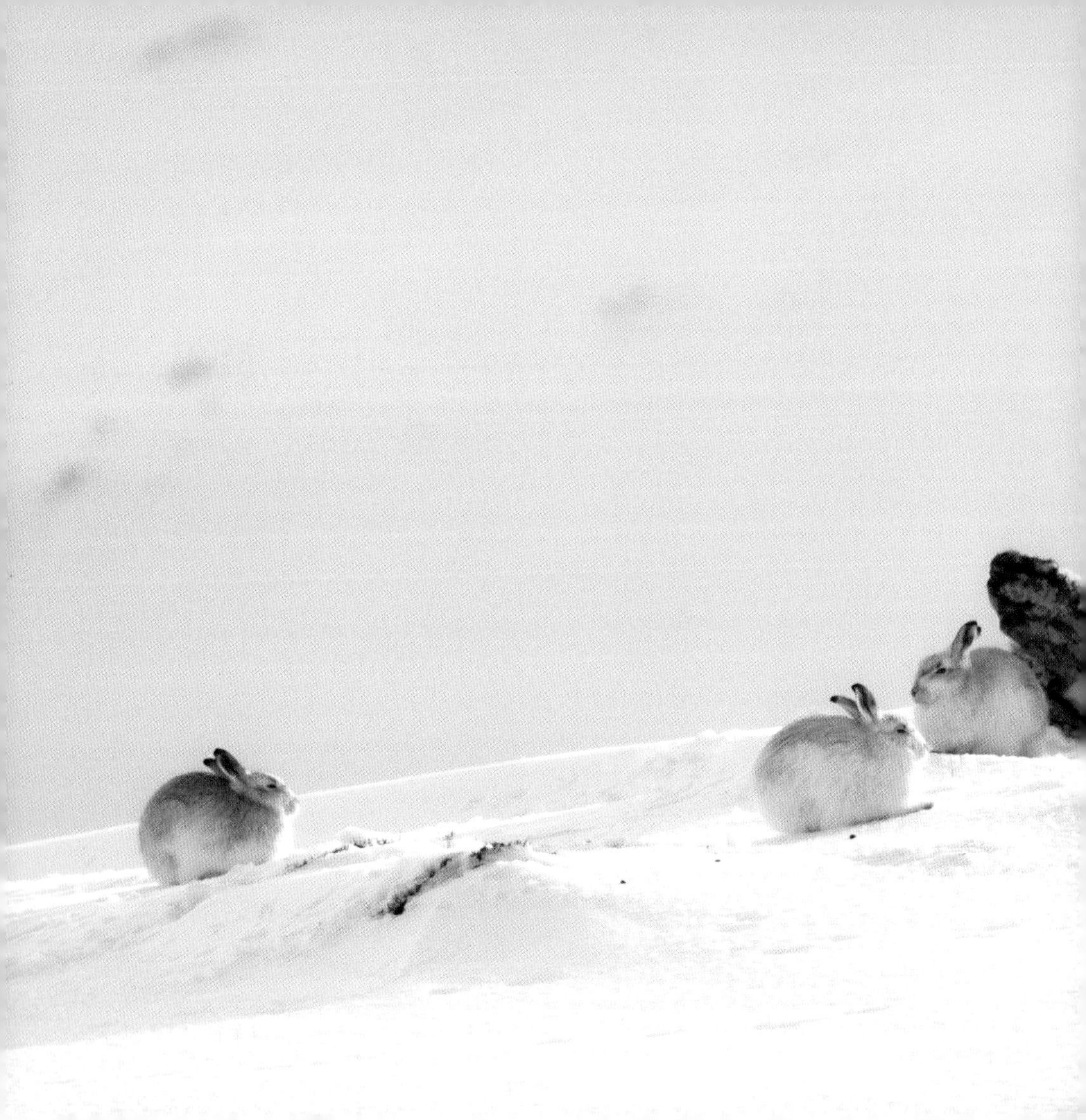

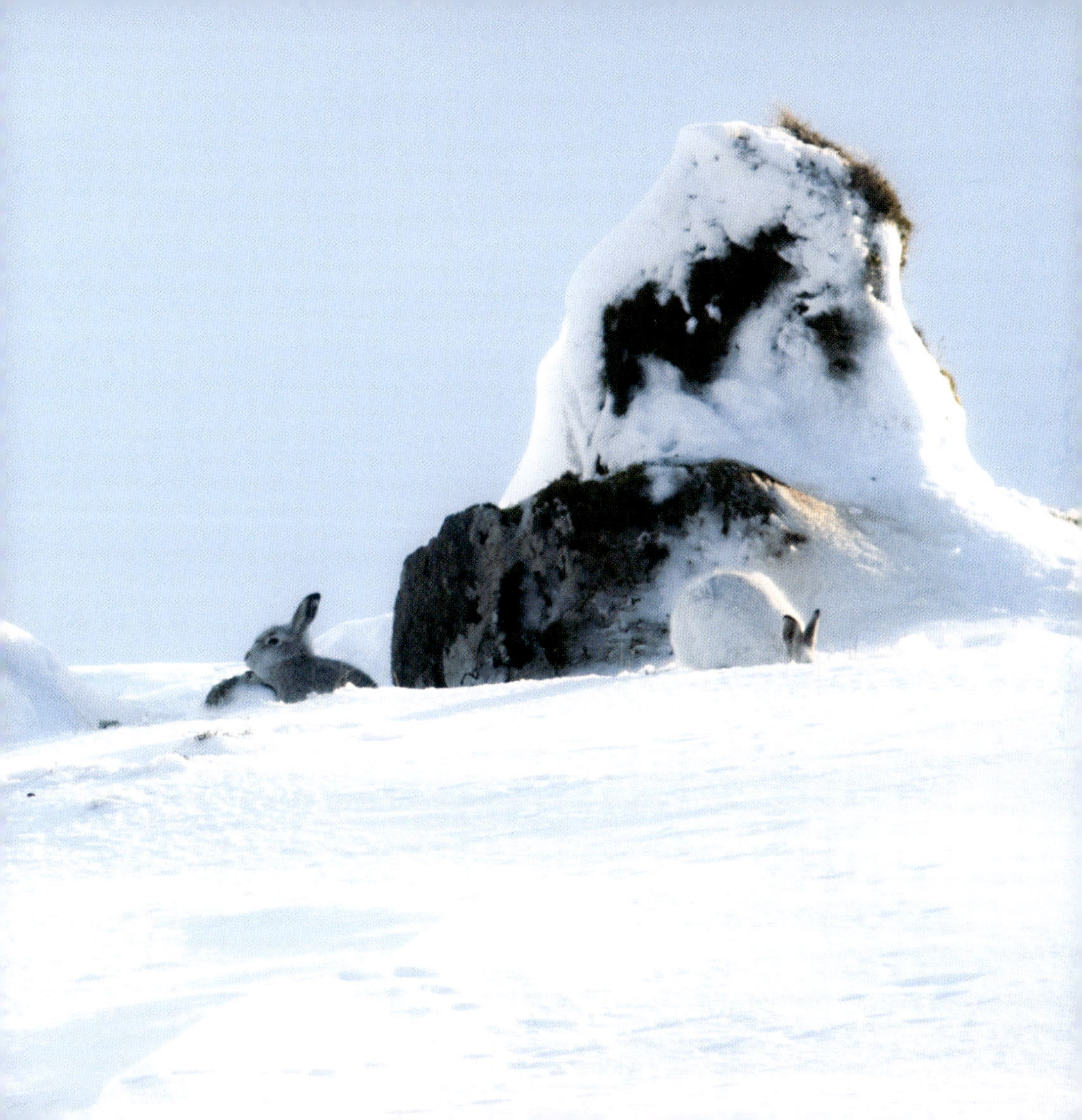

On average, mountain hares live for three to four years.

During periods of snow cover they gather on leeward hill slopes, in groups of 20 or more, to shelter or feed where shallow snow permits scraping to reveal underlying heather. Their 'runs' can be clearly seen through the undergrowth on a mountainside, usually passing directly up slopes; short front legs and long very powerful back legs proving the perfect engine for speed (up to 60km per hour) in uphill terrain. Sheep and deer paths, by contrast, are deeper, wider and traverse across any slope.

The Mammal Society is quoted as saying that mountain hare leverets are preyed upon by several predators including foxes, stoats, cats, buzzards, osprey and eagles; eagles are also major predators of adult hares. On average, mountain hares live for three to four years.

The Scottish mountain hare population was estimated to be around 350,000 in 1995, although this figure is hotly disputed and could be as much as 50 per cent over or under. Population densities are known to vary at least ten fold, reaching a peak approximately every ten years. The reasons for these fluctuations are unclear but may possibly be related to parasite burdens.

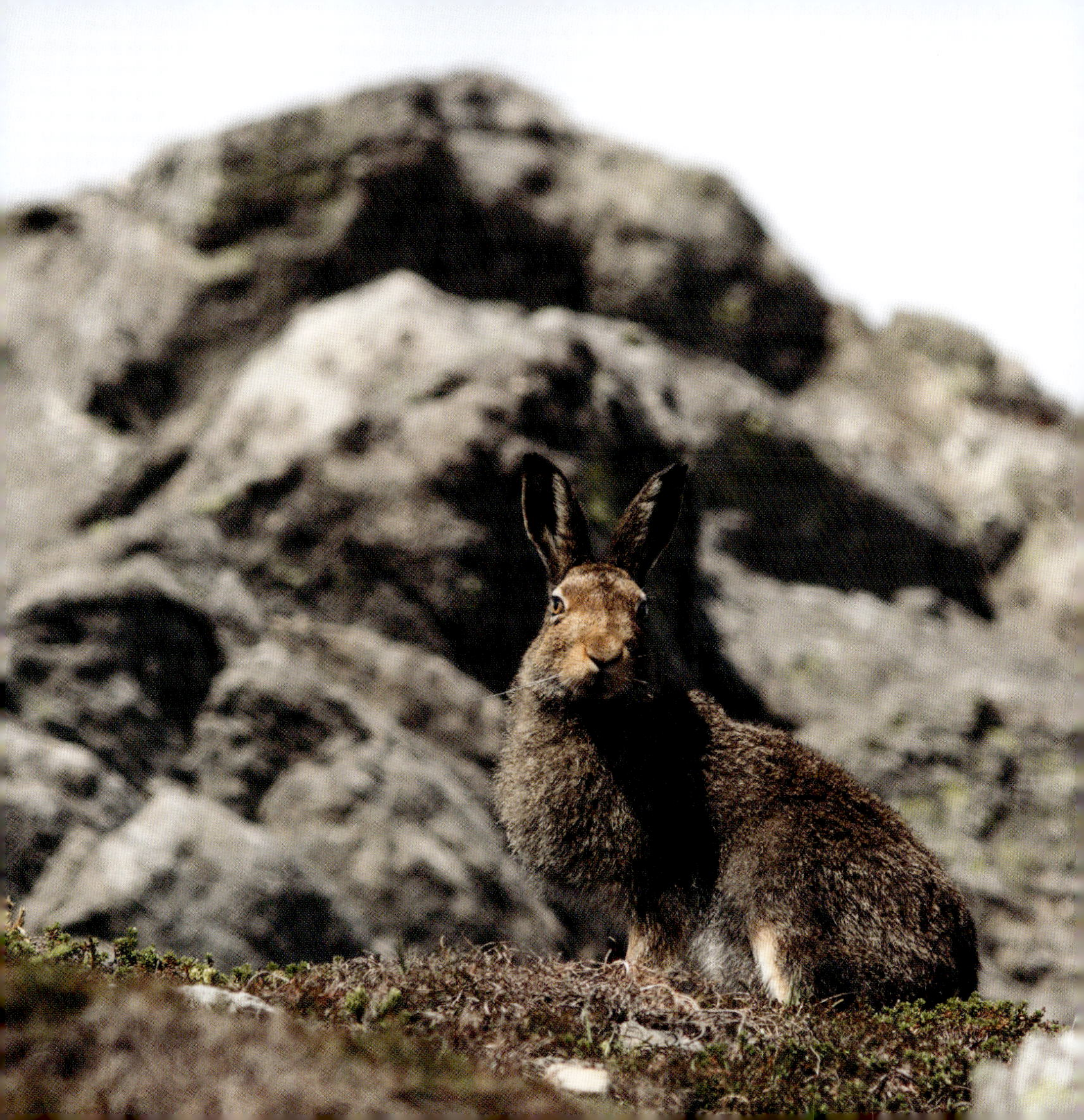

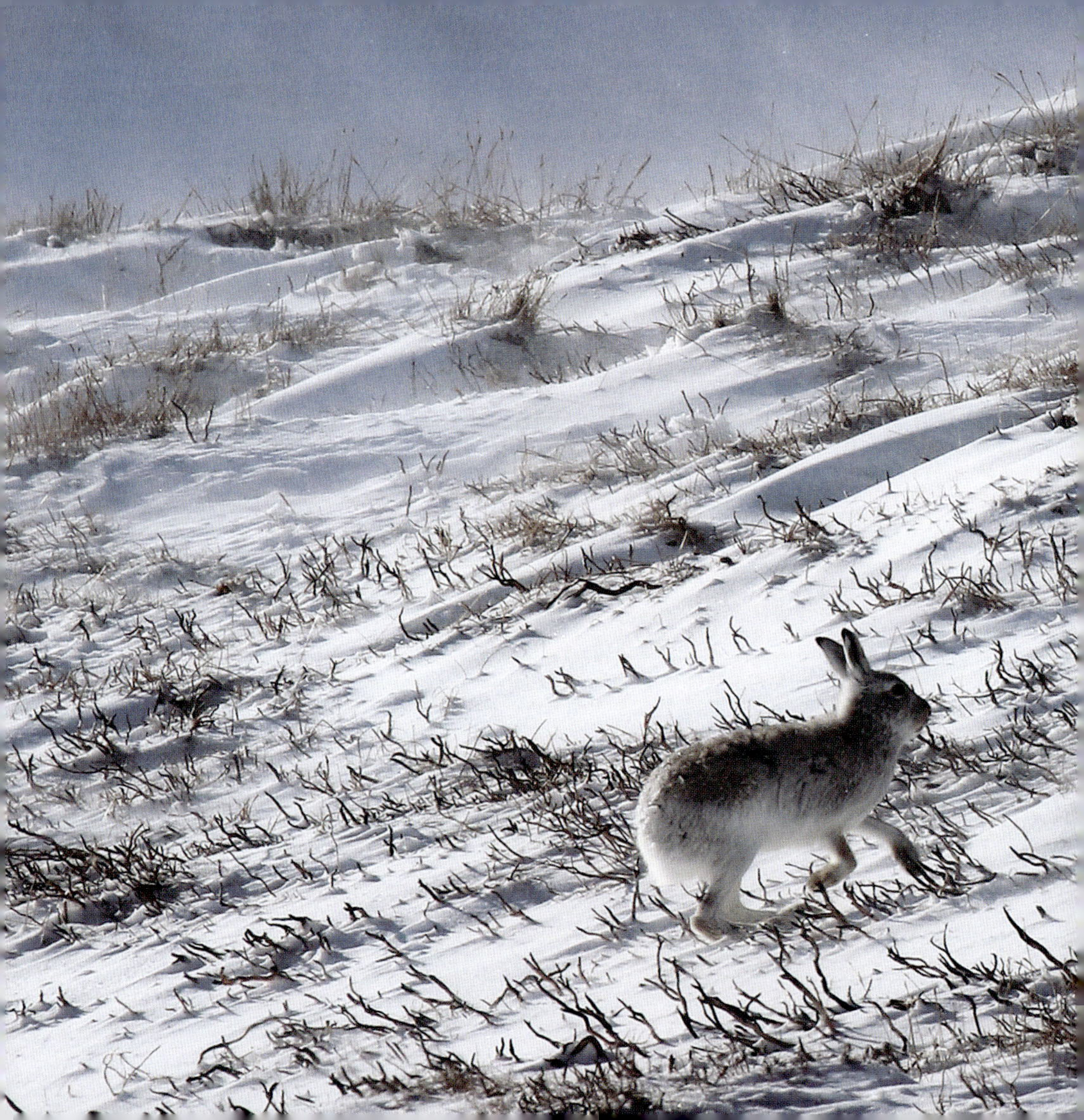

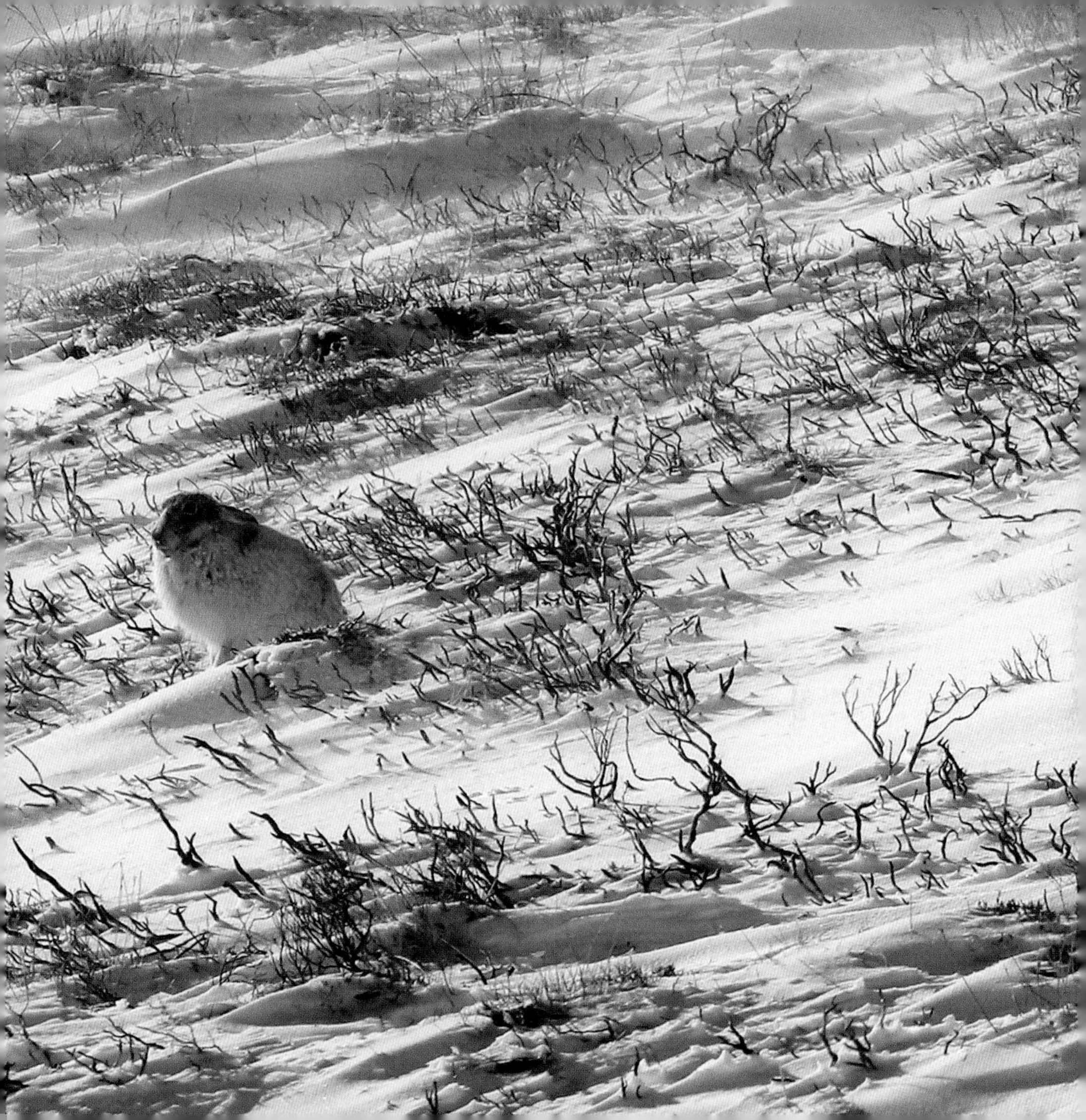

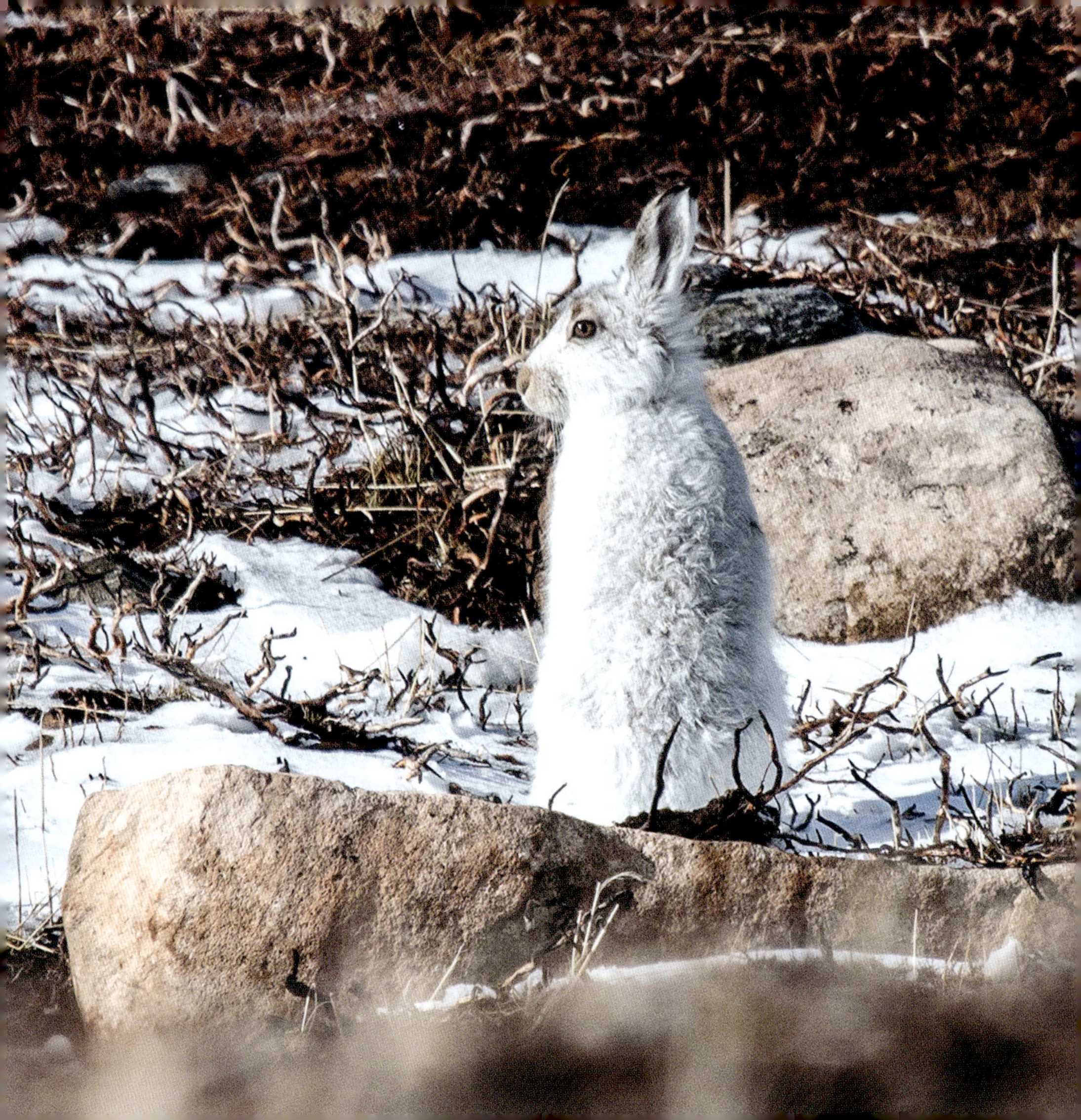

Most leverets are born between March and August inclusive.

Mating begins at the end of January and pregnancy lasts about 50 days. Most leverets are born between March and August inclusive.

There is increasing concern about the status of the mountain hare with reports of it being virtually extinct in some parts of Scotland where it was previously abundant. In some areas excessive grazing by deer, sheep and cattle have depleted the heather so that less food and cover is available for the hares. However, they have also declined on moorland devoid of deer and sheep, leading to the conclusion that human interference is responsible for the decline.

Close season: the Scottish Parliament has instigated close seasons in Scotland for the mountain hare (1st March to 31st July). There is no close season in England.

Mountain hares are listed in Annex V of the EC Habitats Directive (1992), as 'a species of community interest whose taking in the wild and exploitation may be subject to management measures'. This conservation status means that certain methods of capture are prohibited or restricted.

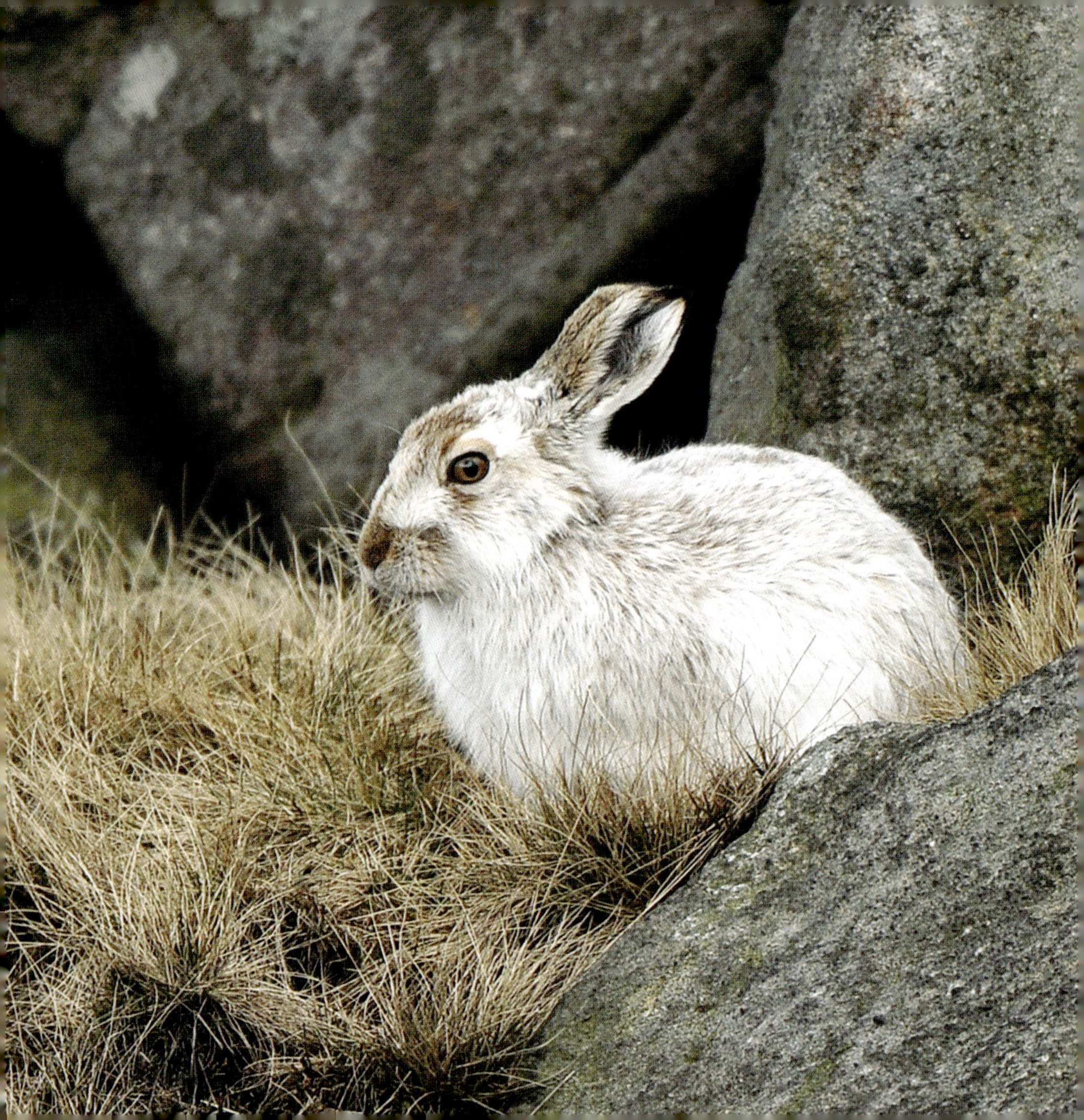

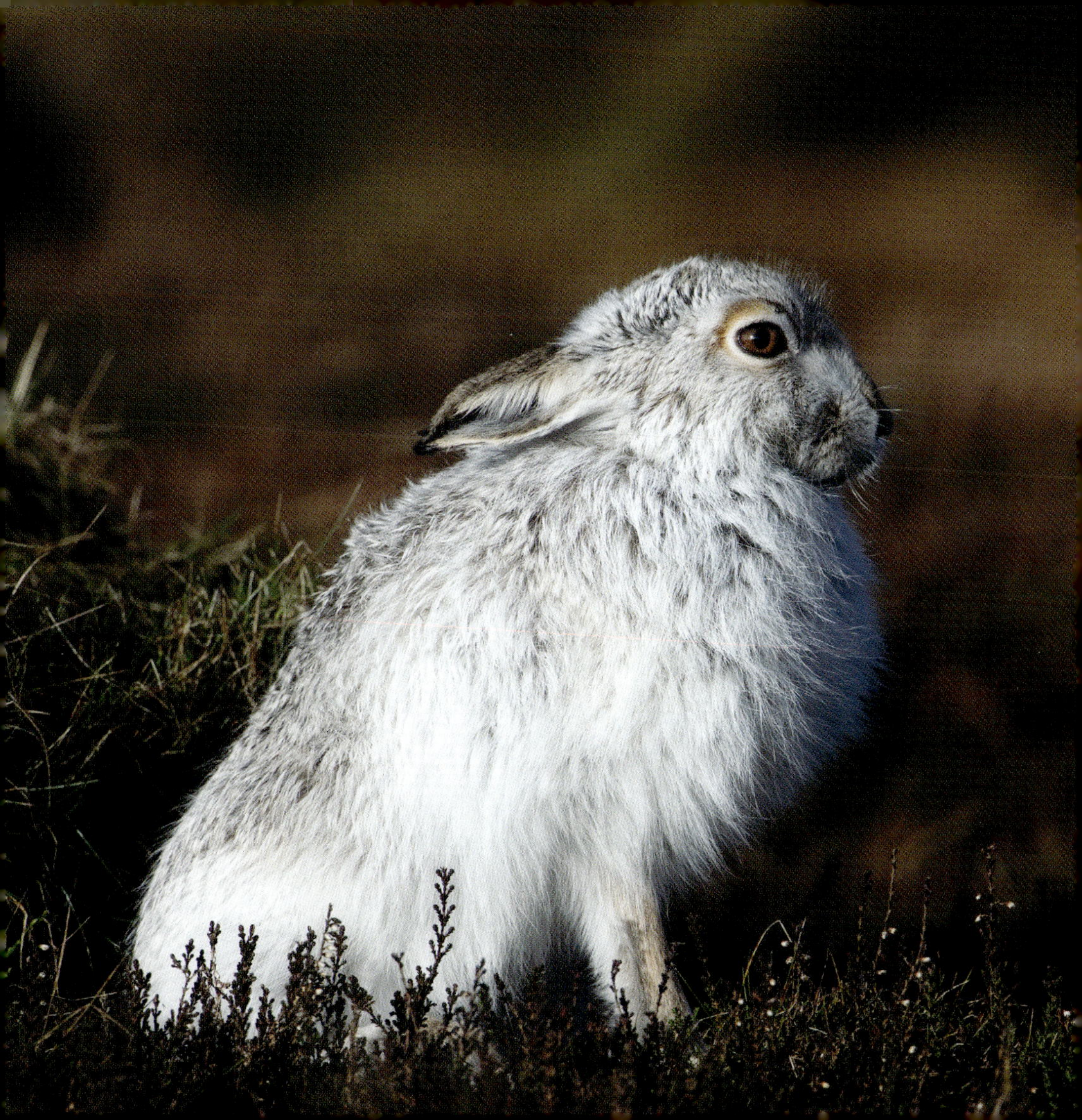

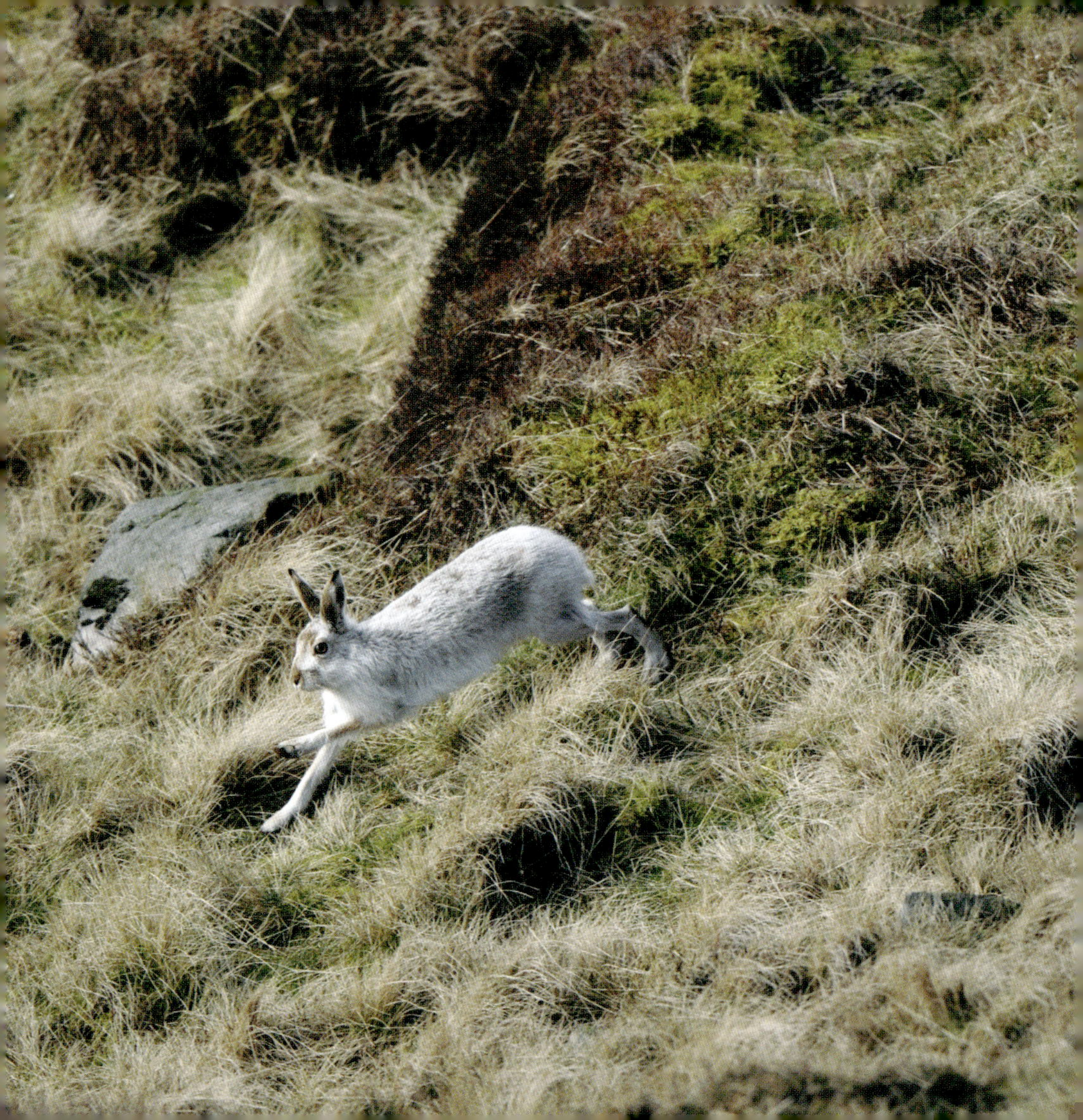

There are few things in the countryside more exciting than catching sight of a mountain hare peering over the snow.

While the mountain hare is persecuted directly for sport it is also snared and shot in large numbers because it allegedly carries a tic-borne virus which kills grouse chicks and is therefore seen as a threat to the grouse shooting industry. The Habitats Directive requires member states to ensure exploitation of Annex V species is 'compatible with their being maintained at a favourable conservation status'. Since there are no official records of the number of hares being killed it is difficult to see how this requirement can be met. But anecdotal evidence of culling levels strongly suggests that EC wildlife law is being broken in Scotland. The British Trust for Ornithology, which also monitors the increase/decrease in the population of certain mammal species, recorded a 43 per cent decline in the number of mountain hare sightings during the period 1995 to 2012. Even allowing for the cyclical nature of their breeding pattern, if this trend were to continue the implications for the mountain hare could be very serious indeed.

There are few things in the countryside more exciting than catching sight of a mountain hare peering over the snow. In the depths of winter, they are harbingers of the spring life to come.

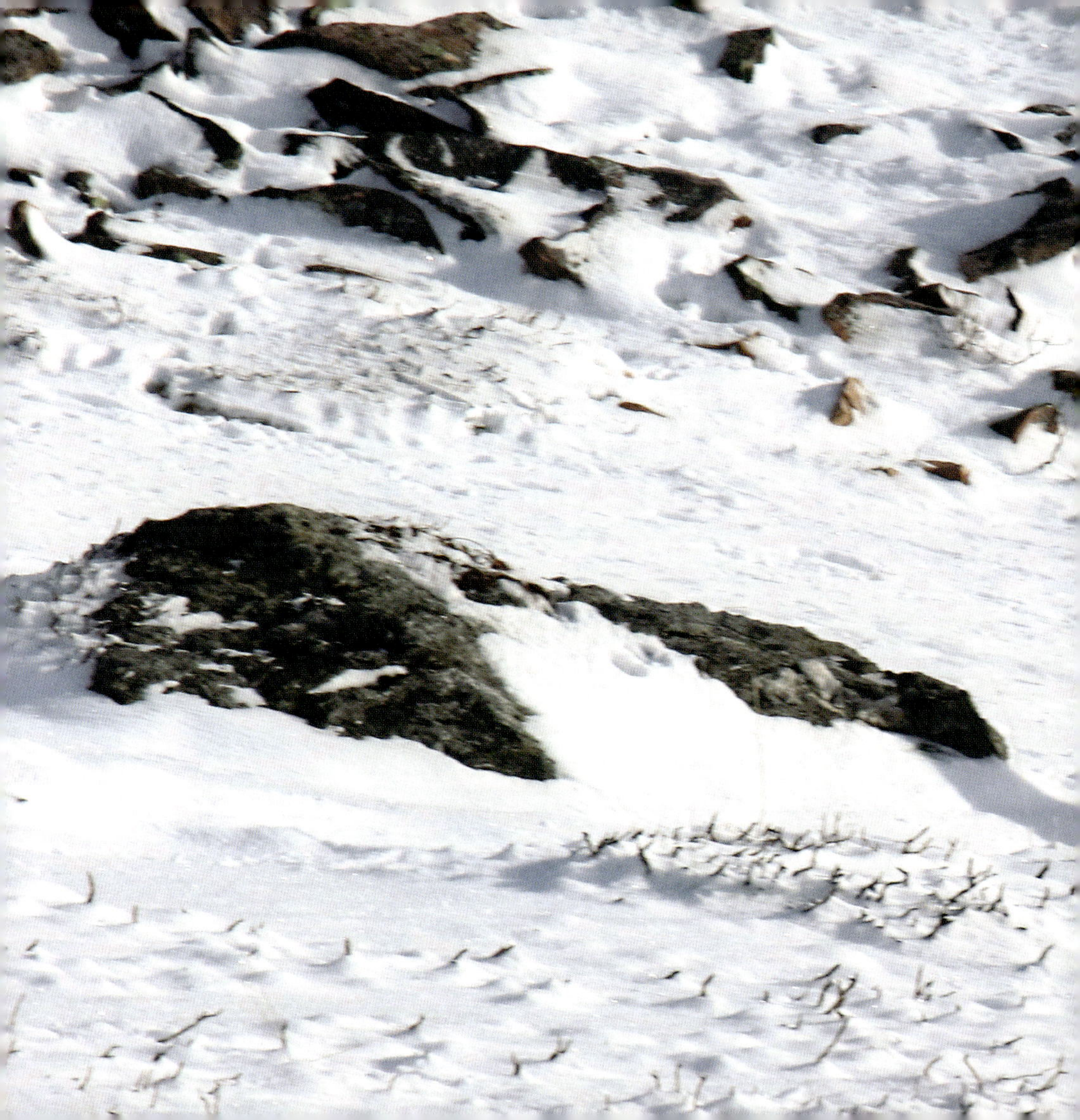

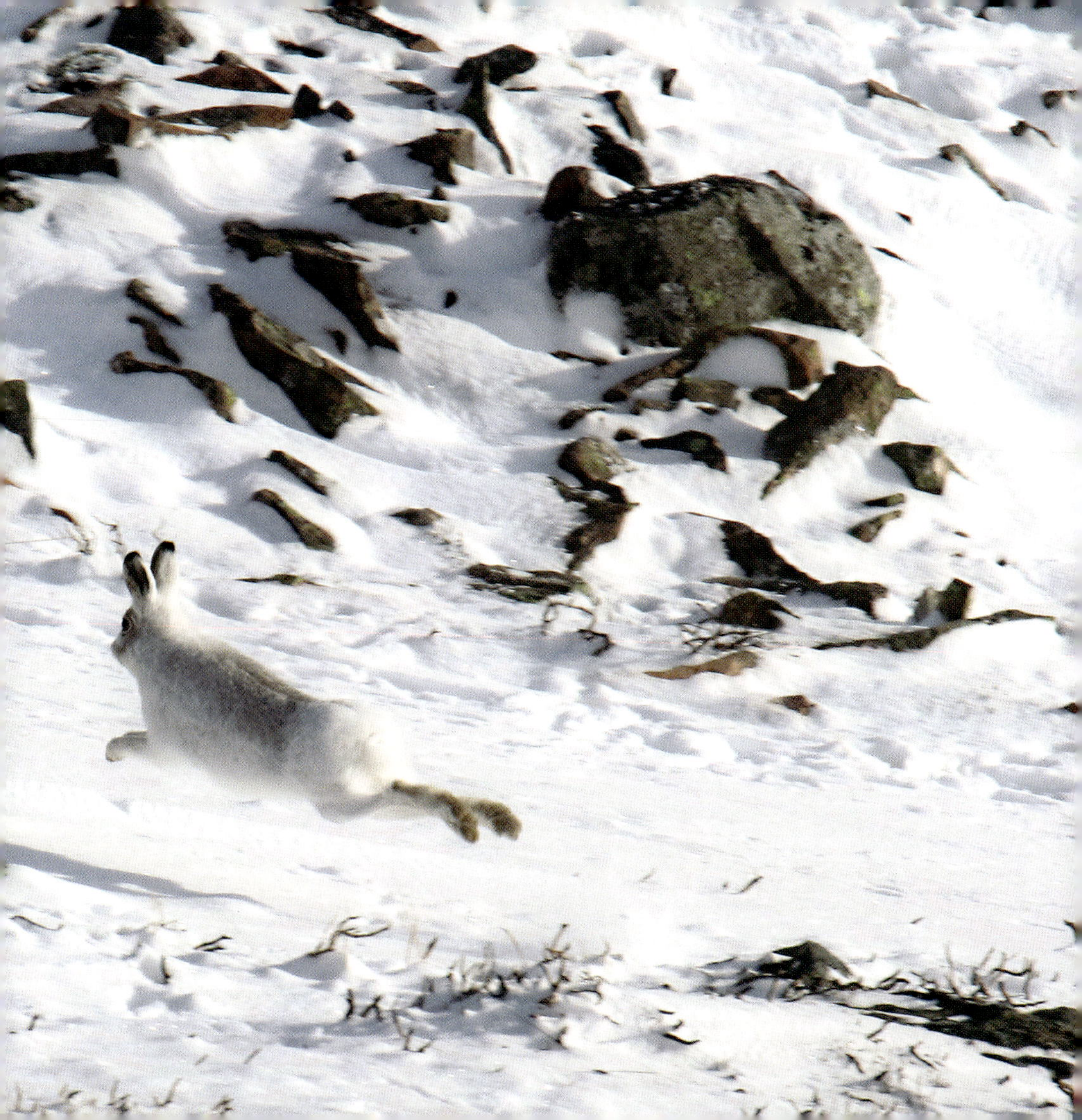

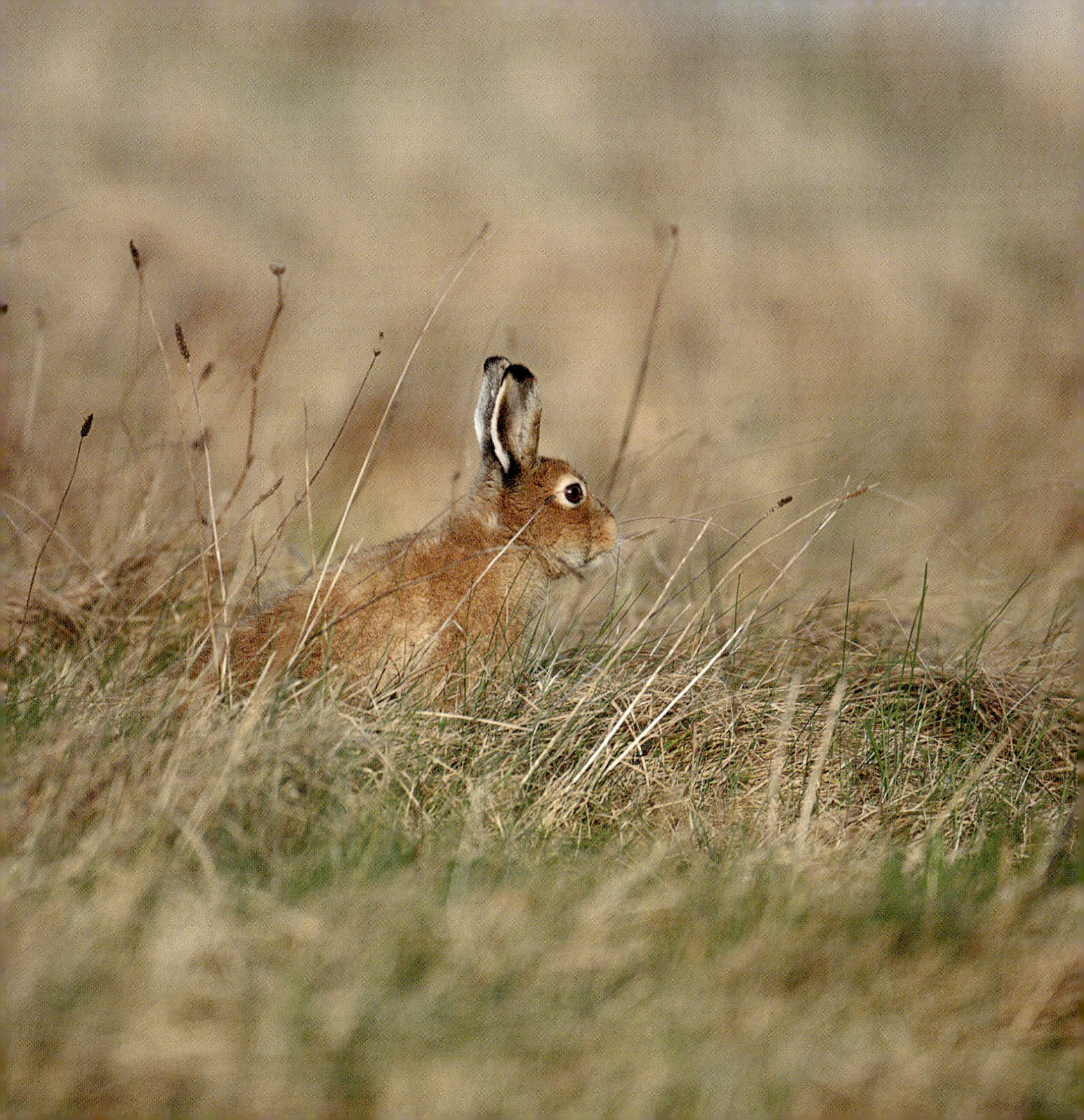

The Irish hare
Lepus timidus hibernicus

This species is Ireland's only native hare and may be found throughout the Irish mainland and on some offshore islands. Although historically classed as a subspecies of the British mountain hare (Lepus timidus scoticus), DNA research has revealed it to be genetically distinct from its British cousins. This is a feature of island groups that have remained isolated from general populations for long periods of time.

Fossil evidence shows that Irish hares were present in Ireland as far back as 30,000 BC. During the most recent ice age, which started in 78,000 BC and reached its maximum 20,000 BC, an ice free, tundra-like landscape covered the southern part of Ireland from Kerry to Waterford. Also, around 18,000 BC, the sea level was about 140 metres lower than at present. The area now covered by the Celtic Sea and English Channel would have consisted of relatively ice-free dry land. These areas appear to have offered a refuge for the Irish hare in which it was able to survive. This makes the Irish hare arguably the oldest living Irish mammal species.

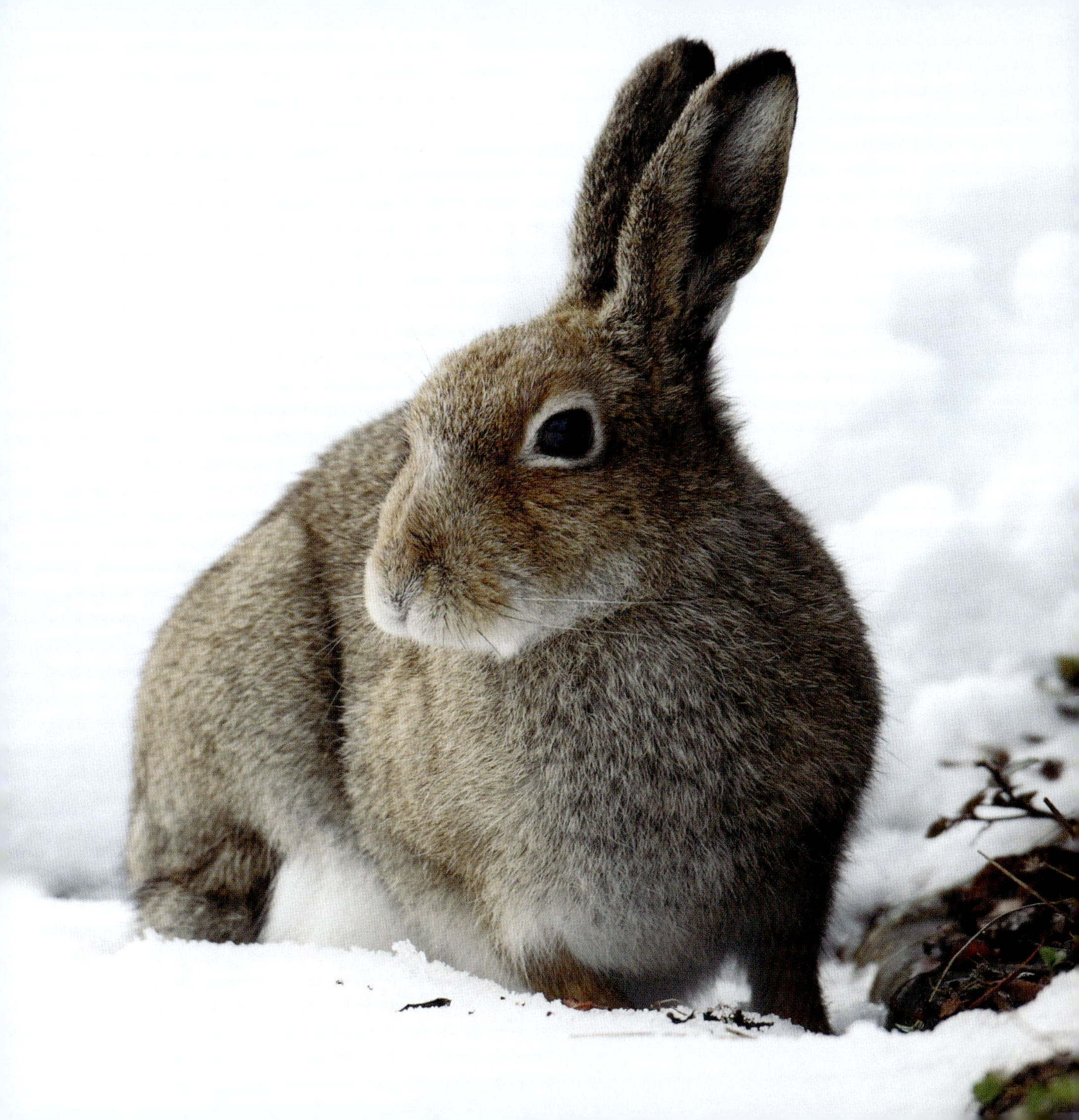

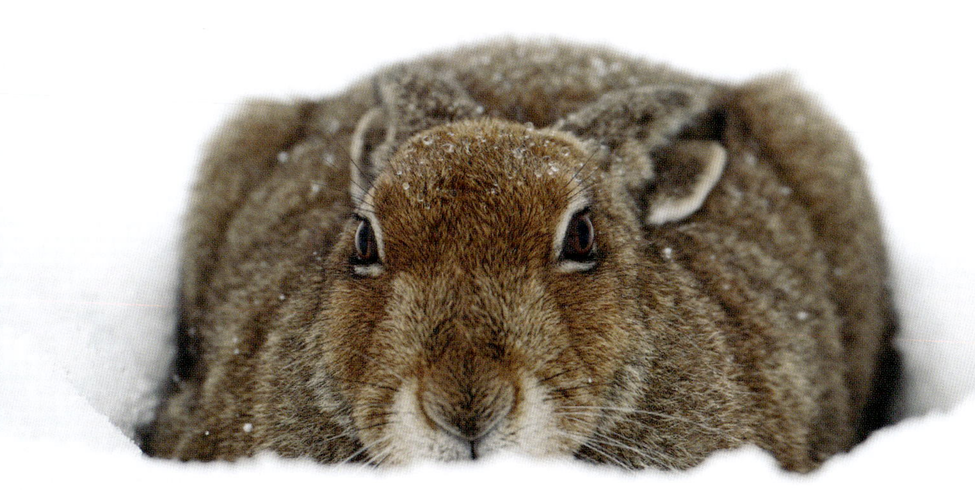

Fur (pelage) colour varies widely in Irish hares and can range from a light 'blond' through brown to the russet red described in textbooks. The coat, however, whilst not normally turning white in winter, can become lighter and greyer. There are two moults and the coat can vary throughout the year, developing white patches. Rarely, some all-white specimens have been known and gained a place in folklore. White colouring is usually associated with high altitudes during winter. However during the extremely cold winter of 2010/2011 a significant number of all-white and partly white hares were reported widely across Ireland.

As with the mountain hare, the black tipped ears are smaller than the brown hare's and would not reach the tip of the nose if pulled forward. Although tail colour is often quoted in texts as white on both surfaces, Irish hares may also sport a black upper tail surface similar to that found on brown (European) hares. Consequently, fur and tail colour of Irish hares may not be reliable characteristics for identification. The wide range of fur colouring (sometimes brown) and occasional black tails may lead those individuals to be mistaken for brown hares.

A now famous genetic variant is the Golden Hare of Rathlin Island, a small island just off the north coast of County Antrim.

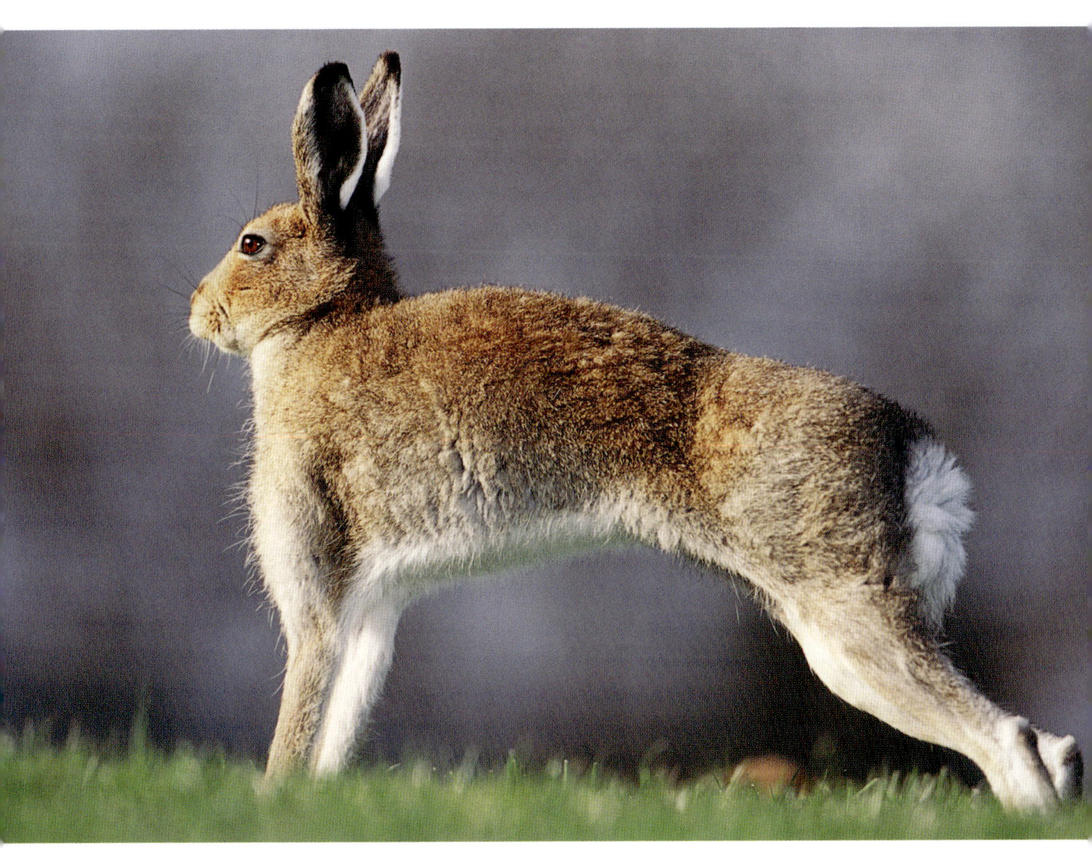

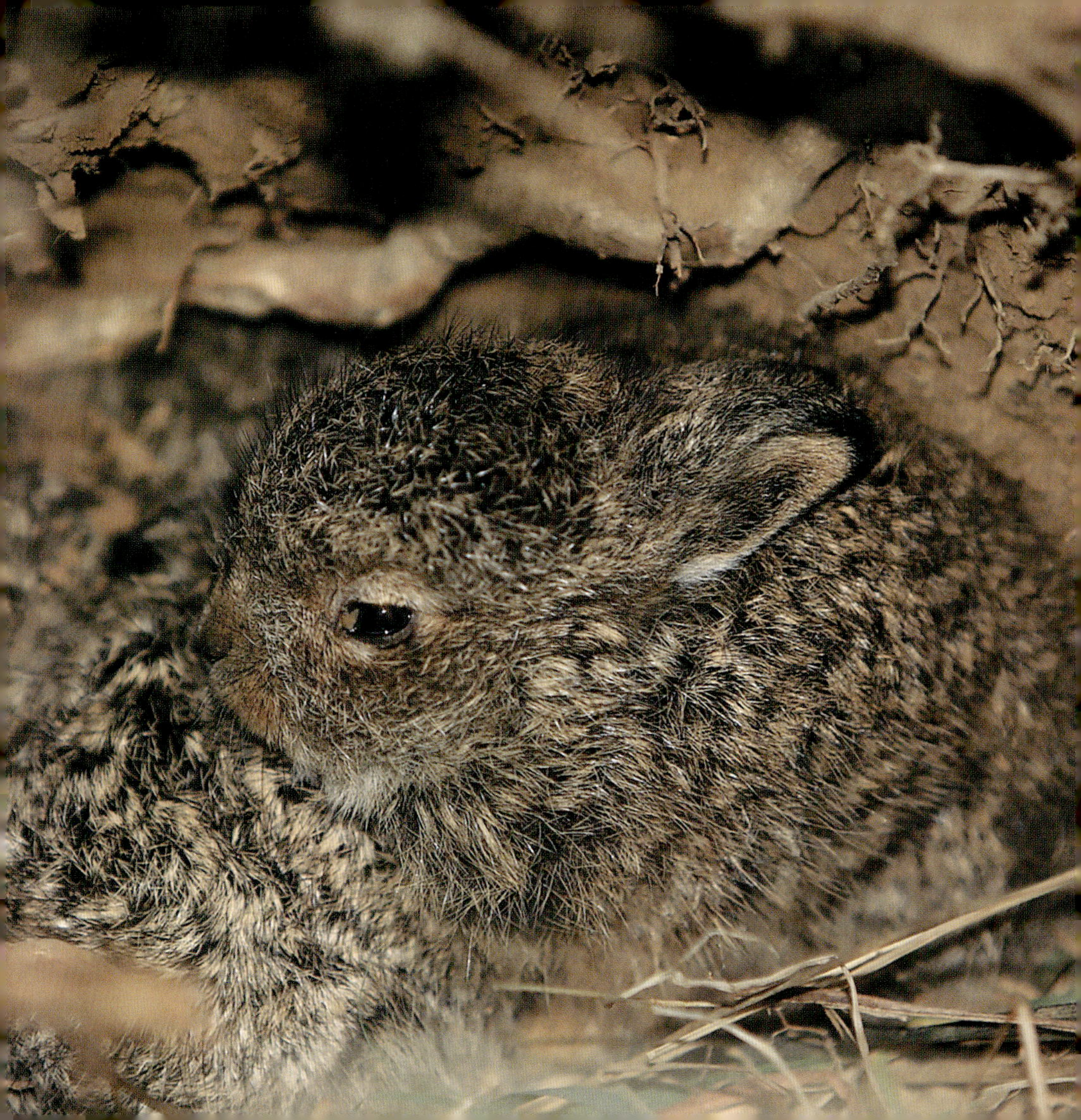

Although named after its 'golden' fur colour the really unique feature of this animal is its blue eyes. This is a product of yet further isolation from the general population on the Irish mainland. Golden hares are erythristic (albino) individuals and not typical of the general hare population on Rathlin Island.

Although native only to Ireland, some Irish hares have been recorded on Mull and are thought to be descendants of hares introduced from Ireland during the 19th century.

The animals have long powerful back legs that help them reach speeds of up to 30mph/50kph and jump heights of around two metres. They feed mainly on a variety of grasses but sedges, heather, wild thyme, bilberry and even the shoots of young trees may also play an important part in their diet, depending on the habitat. Irish hares have also been reported grazing on seaweed. Like the brown and mountain hares, Irish hares do not live in a burrow underground but shelter in a hollow depression above ground known as a form.

Courtship and mating, the leaping and boxing behaviour which accompanies it, are all as per their English cousins, as is the fact that young are born fully furred, have their eyes open and wean for at least four weeks.

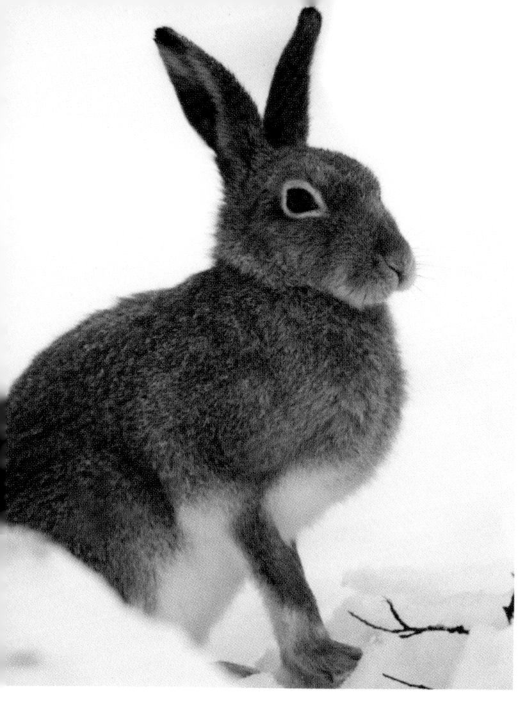

mortality rate of up to 75 per cent in the first year and their average life expectancy is thought to be around three years.

Irish hares occur in a wide range of habitats and at all altitudes, including lowland raised bogs, blanket bog, grasslands and sand dunes.

Historically the Irish hare was widespread and common throughout Ireland, but population levels have undergone a substantial decline since the mechanisation of grass cutting and latterly with intensive harvesting for silage. Notwithstanding cyclic fluctuations, there is evidence of continuing decline. Irish hares are now reported to be locally

Irish hares are known to breed in at least eleven months of the year, although leverets are more likely to be seen during the summer months. Typically a litter comprises between one and four leverets, with the average being two. Young hares face a

extinct in some areas and well known populations, such as those at Aldergrove near Belfast and Bull Island near Dublin, have also suffered declines. Traditionally the Irish hare has been regarded as a game species in Ireland and may be shot or hunted with dogs during the 'open season'. Hares may not be hunted or taken by any means during the 'close season', which extends from 1st February to 11th August in Northern Ireland and 1st March to 25th September in the Irish Republic. Irish hares may not be hunted at night or on Sundays.

In January 2004, due to concerns about the low numbers of Irish hares, the then Minister of the Environment for Northern Ireland introduced a series of annual temporary protection orders banning the killing, taking, sale or purchase of Irish hares. These continued in 2010. However, they were not renewed, leaving the Irish hare with little protection in law other than restrictions on methods of taking or killing these animals. The Irish hare, as a Priority Species, is now the subject of an All-Ireland Irish Hare Species Action Plan.

Hare coursing was banned in Northern Ireland in 2010 but is legal in the Irish Republic. Often cited as a 'traditional Irish pastime', coursing as practised in Ireland was introduced to the island by the British Army in 1803. The rules of enclosed or park coursing, as it is known, date back to Elizabeth I.

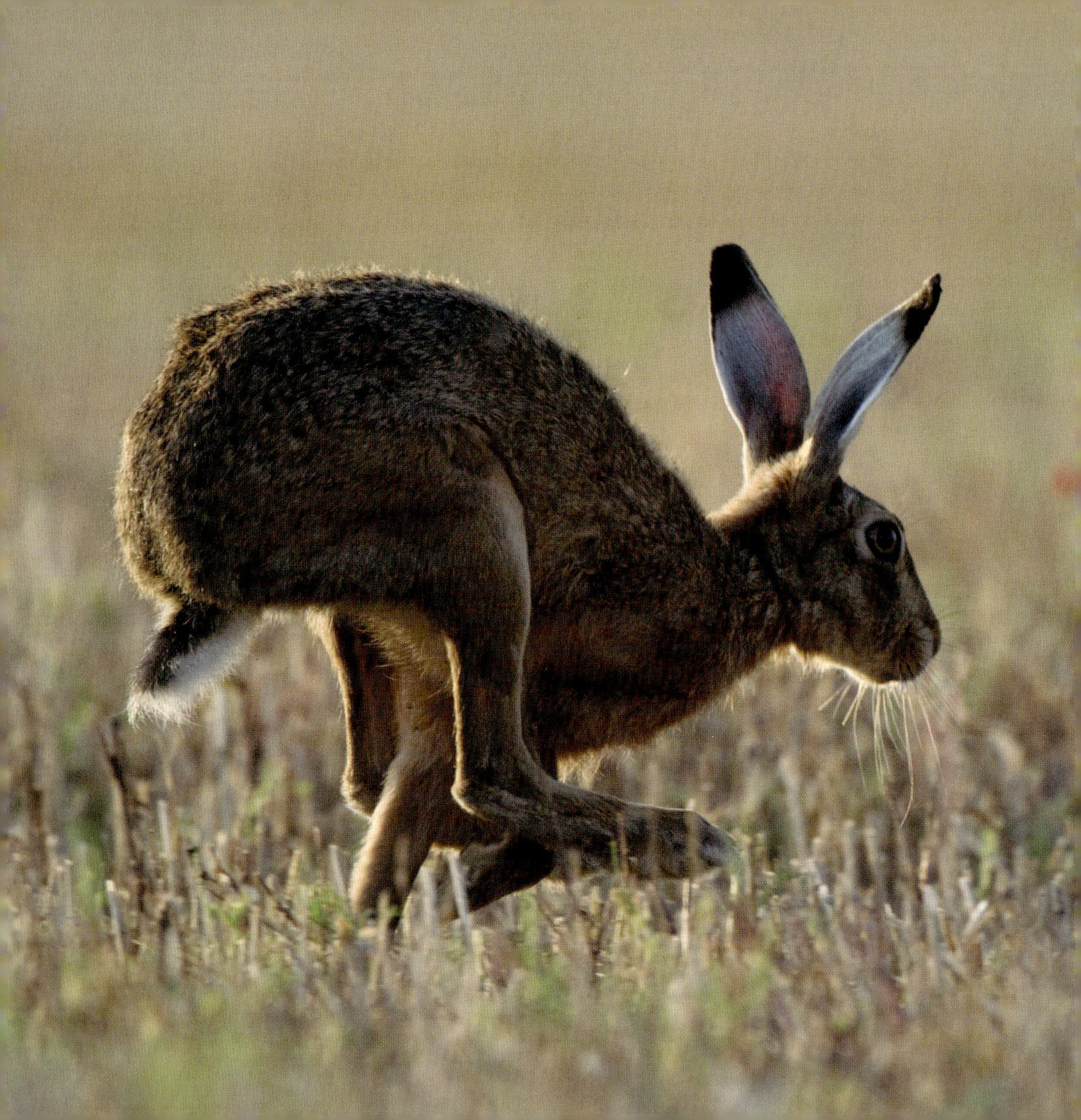

The hare in danger

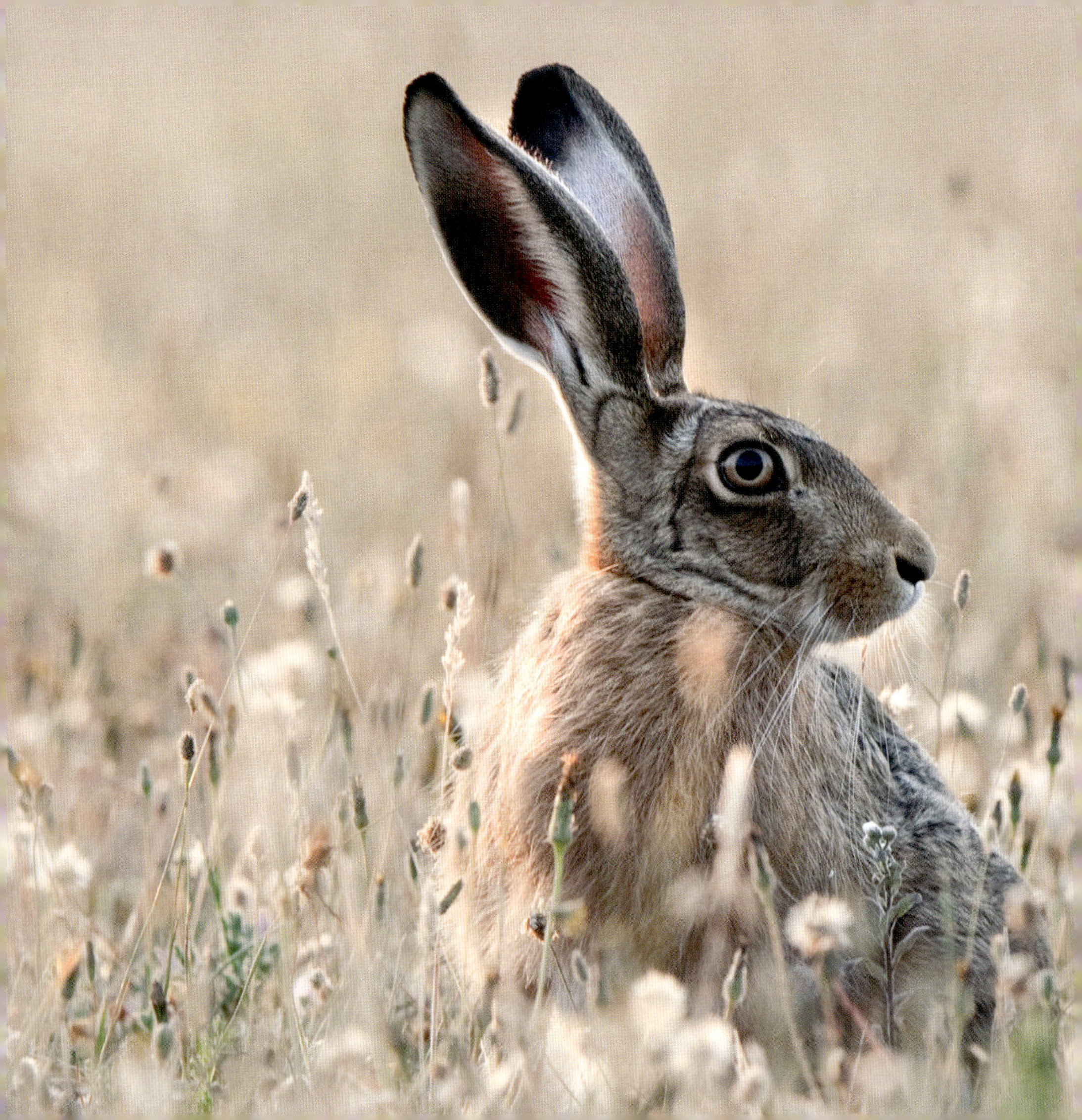

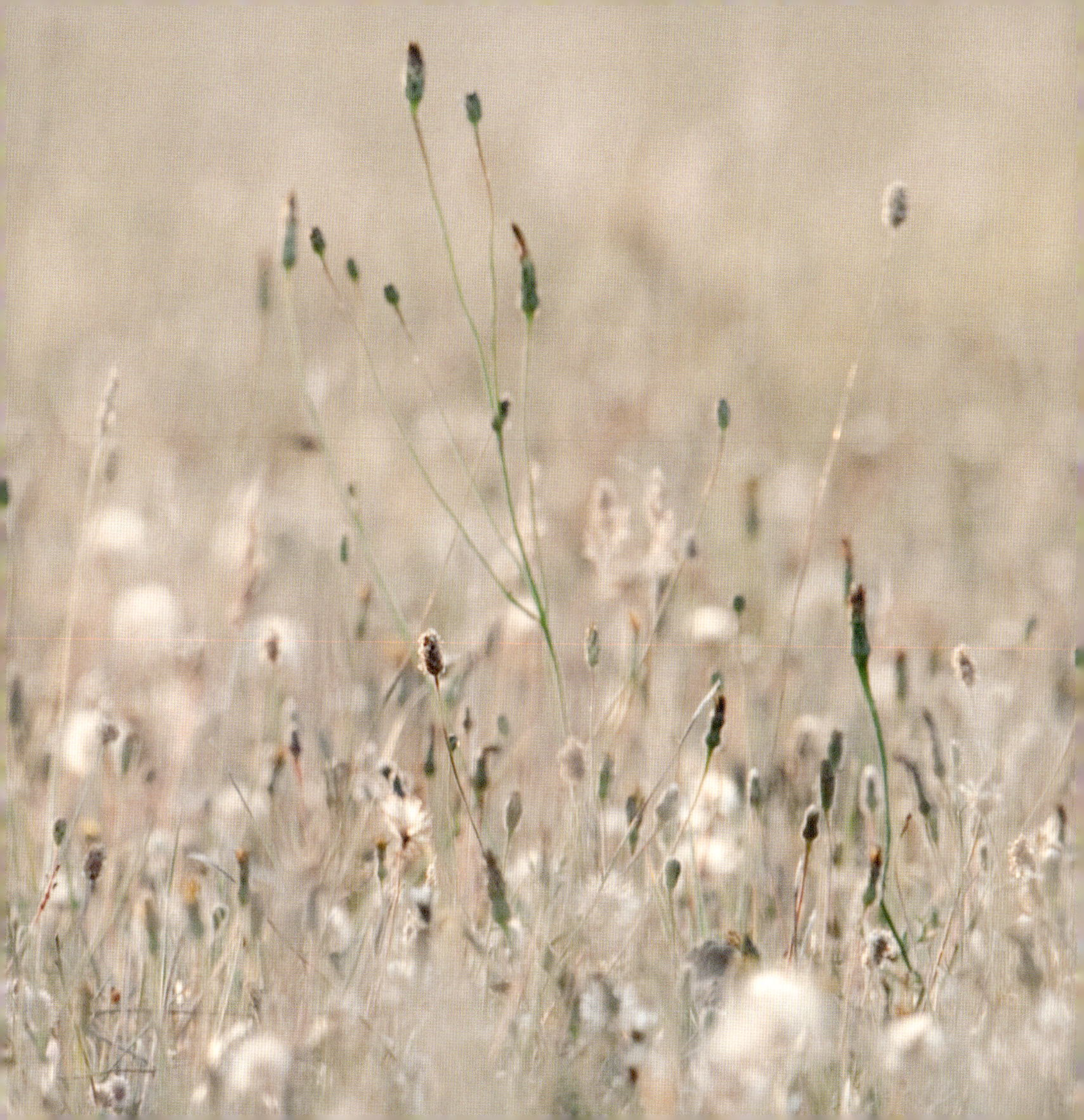

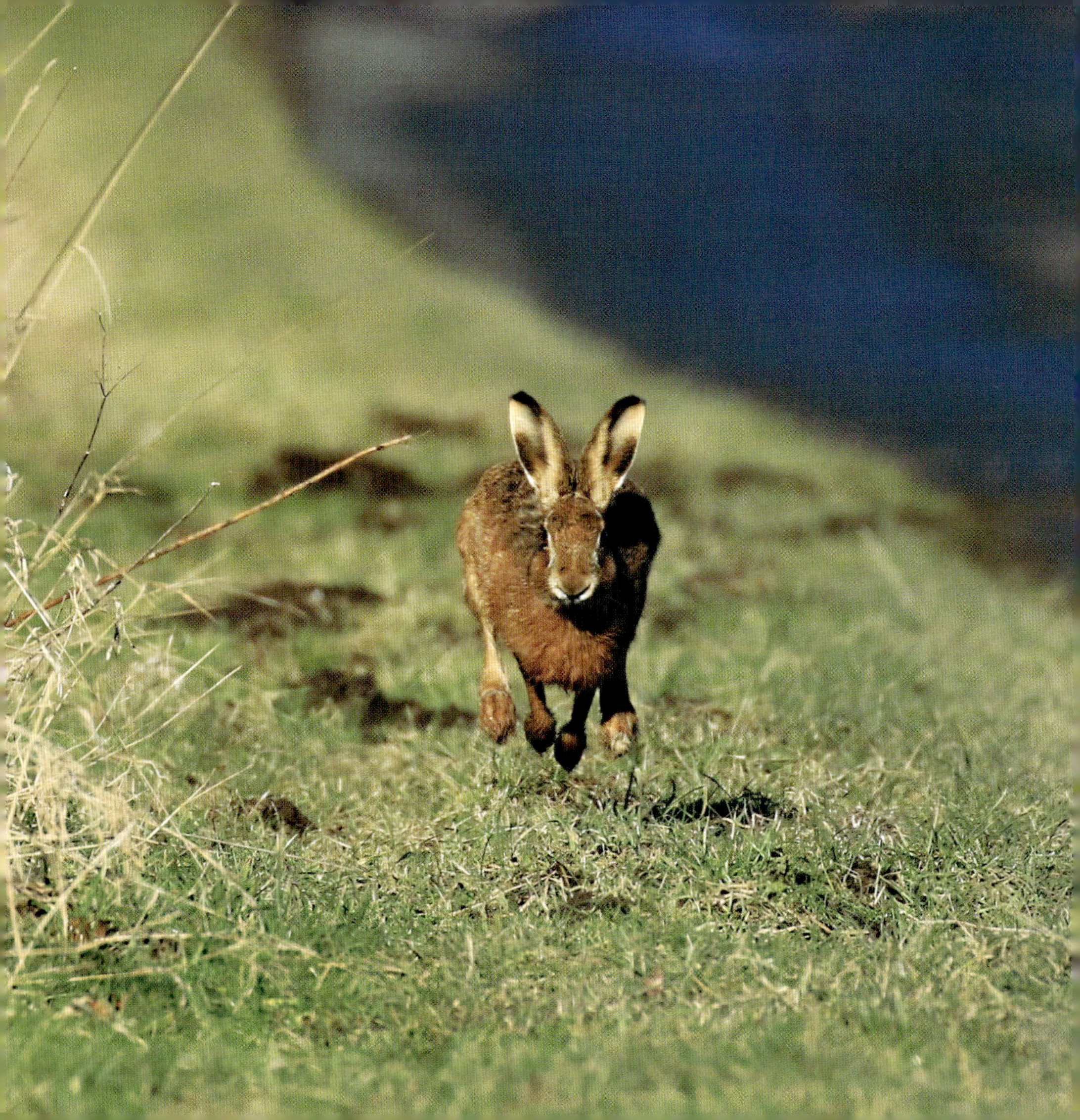

The hare in danger

There are three main reasons why hare numbers have dropped dramatically in the last 100 years:

1. Changes in the agricultural landscape

95 per cent of hay meadows have been lost in the last 50 years. Hay has been replaced by silage, and grassland for forage silage tends to be sown to a reduced number of grass species, resulting in landscapes poor in biodiversity. Despite this, hares fare best in the arable areas of the east of England, giving a marked east–west divide in their national population. Preparation of fields for planting of spring crops can threaten young leverets that will not escape as they habitually 'sit tight'. Later in the year, this 'sit tight' attitude can have an effect on survival numbers of leverets who, if they are using crops for cover, are very vulnerable when fields are harvested, being killed by the forage machinery. Farmers are however being encouraged by various governmental schemes to start cropping from the middle of any given field to help any wildlife escape.

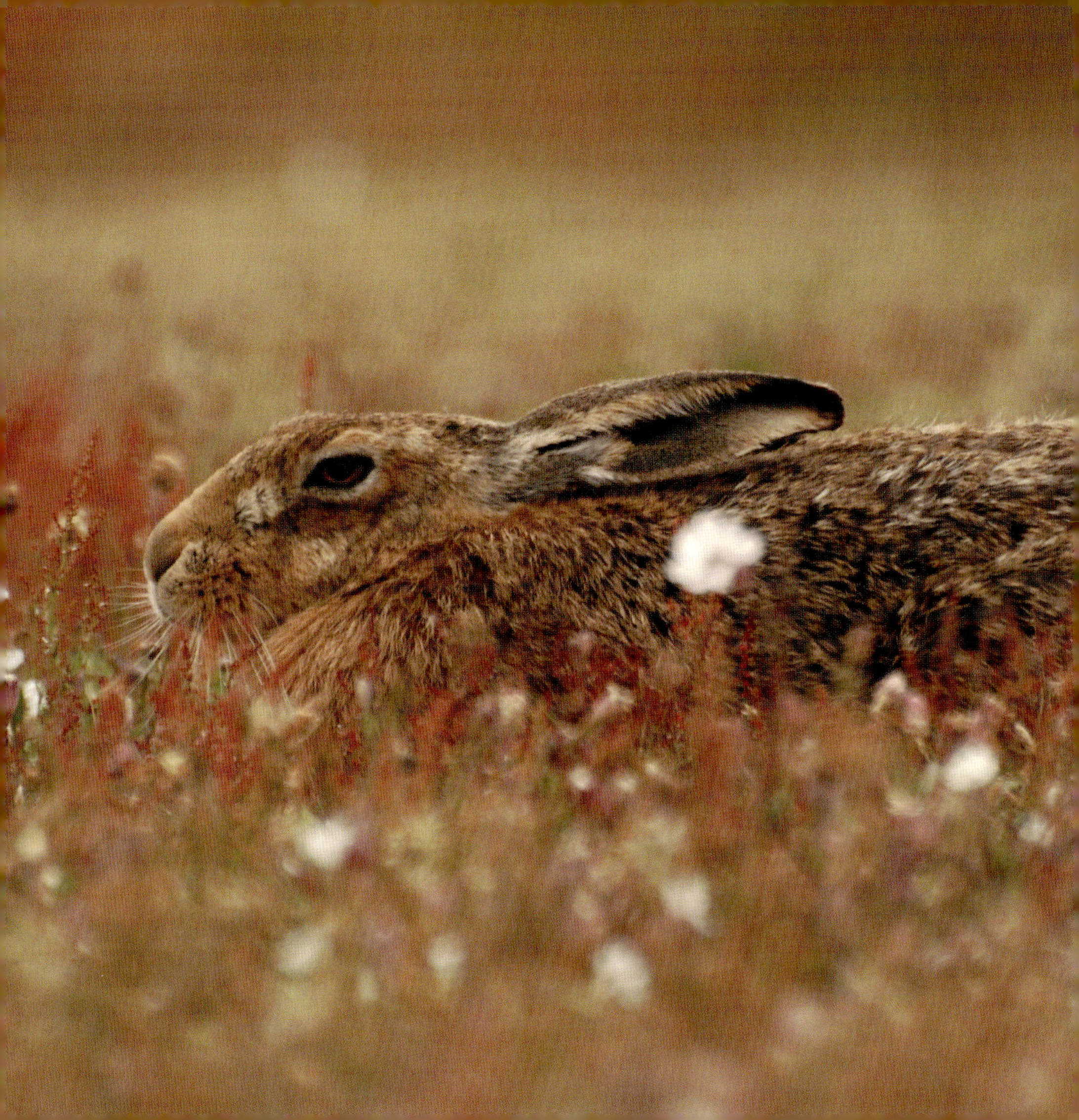

2. Predation

The main predator of the hare is the red fox (*Vulpes vulpes*) and fox predation accounts for 75 to 100 per cent of annual losses in hare populations in southern England. There is a complex balance between predation, habitat quality and land management practices, including management of land through game keeping, which determines the impact of predation and fox numbers on hare populations. Although as previously stated in other chapters, the hare is the UK's fastest mammal and, in a standoff between a hare and a fox, the hare would leave a fox standing; the fox has the upper hand against leverets, and sick or ailing adult hares. Hare numbers are also known to decrease in areas where birds of prey are increasing as not only will raptors take leverets but large birds can also take adults. Crows will attack leverets that are too young to escape, and the HPT even had a report of a leveret running to a woman on a horse for protection when attacked by a crow.

3. Hunting

Most hares are taken by shooting, and organised shoots typically take place in eastern England in February at the end of the pheasant shooting season. Records of the numbers of animals taken have been used as a measure of hare populations and, it is estimated that between

28 and 69 per cent of hares may be removed locally each year by shooting.

Interestingly, despite the key hunting period being in February, game dealer websites indicate that hares are available all year round and prices are at their highest, and demand greatest, from October to December. Game dealers handling hares are widely dispersed throughout Great Britain and it is surprising that the main time of year in which they experience increased supply of hares is late autumn, rather than February, which is the main period for organised shooting.

In addition to organised shooting, illegal poaching using lurchers is known to be a cause of losses in some areas and could have a direct effect on hare numbers, though it is likely to be small. In recent years, since hare coursing has become illegal, landowners and farmers may sometimes shoot and trap hares to reduce the likelihood of trespassing and poaching, which may also affect local populations of hares. Game dealers source hares locally from shooting estates, from other local game dealers, or from the surrounding farms or estates where small numbers may be taken by a farmer and his friends and family on a 'rough shoot' day. Hares may also be imported from countries such as Argentina.

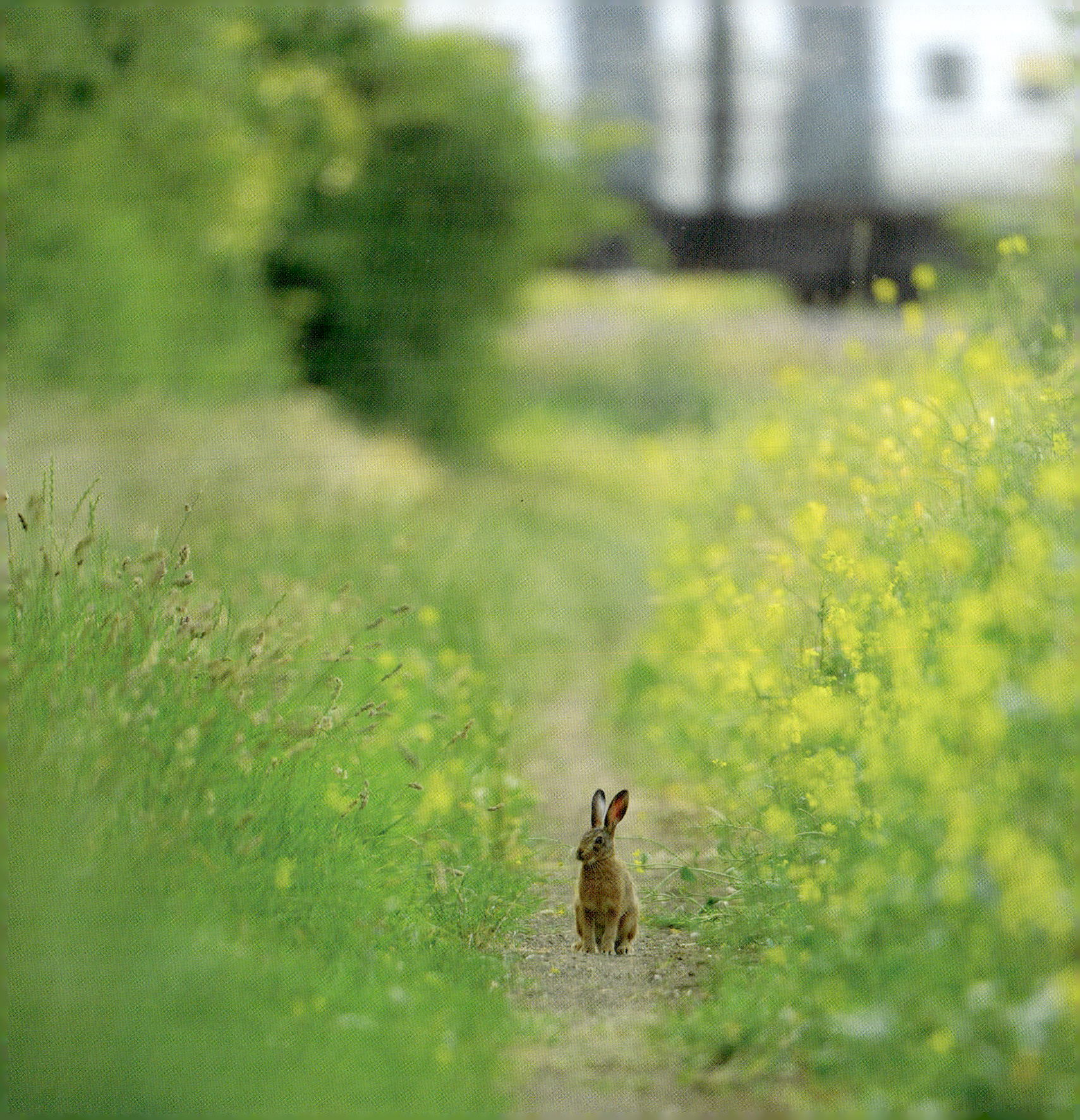

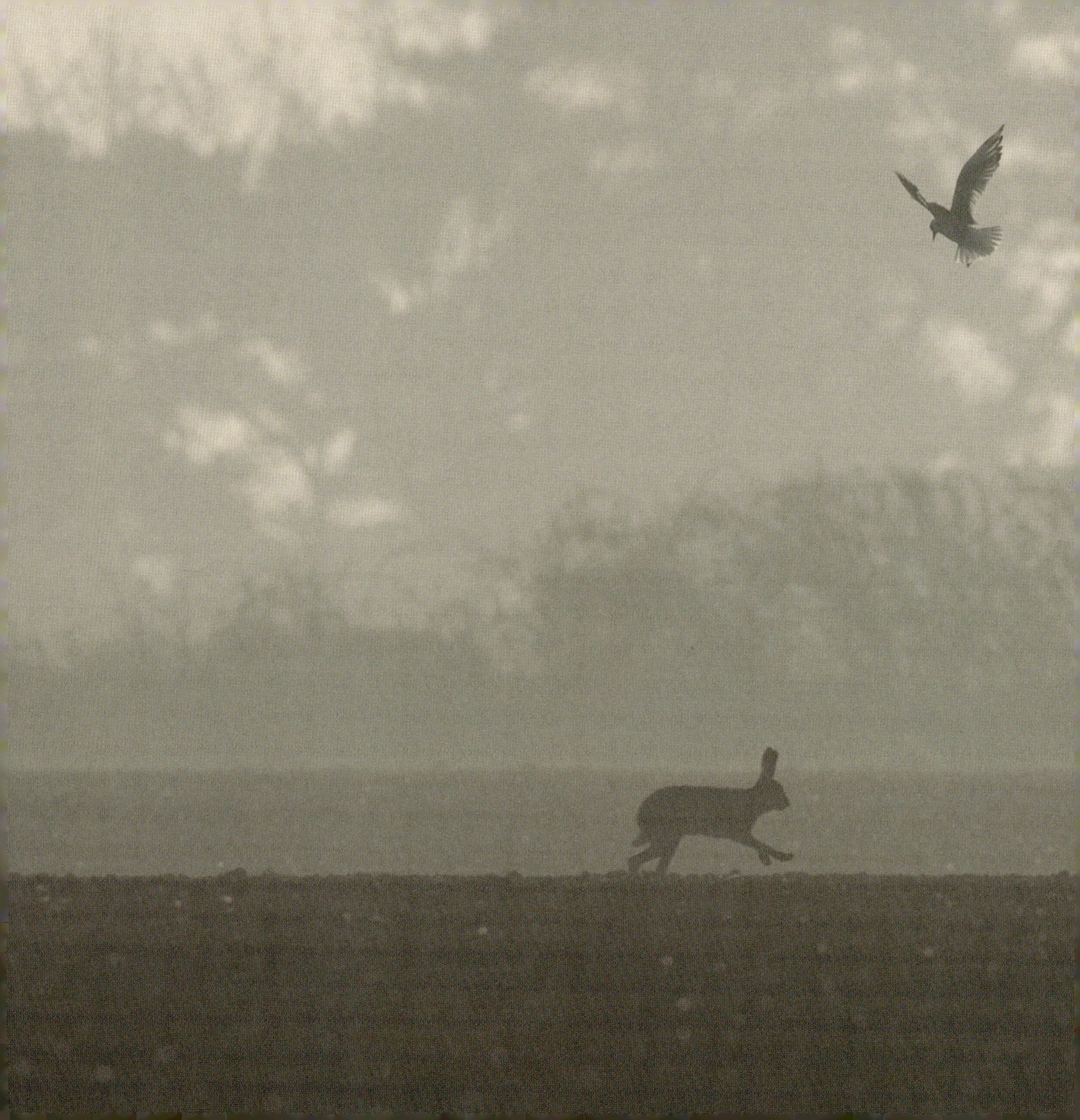

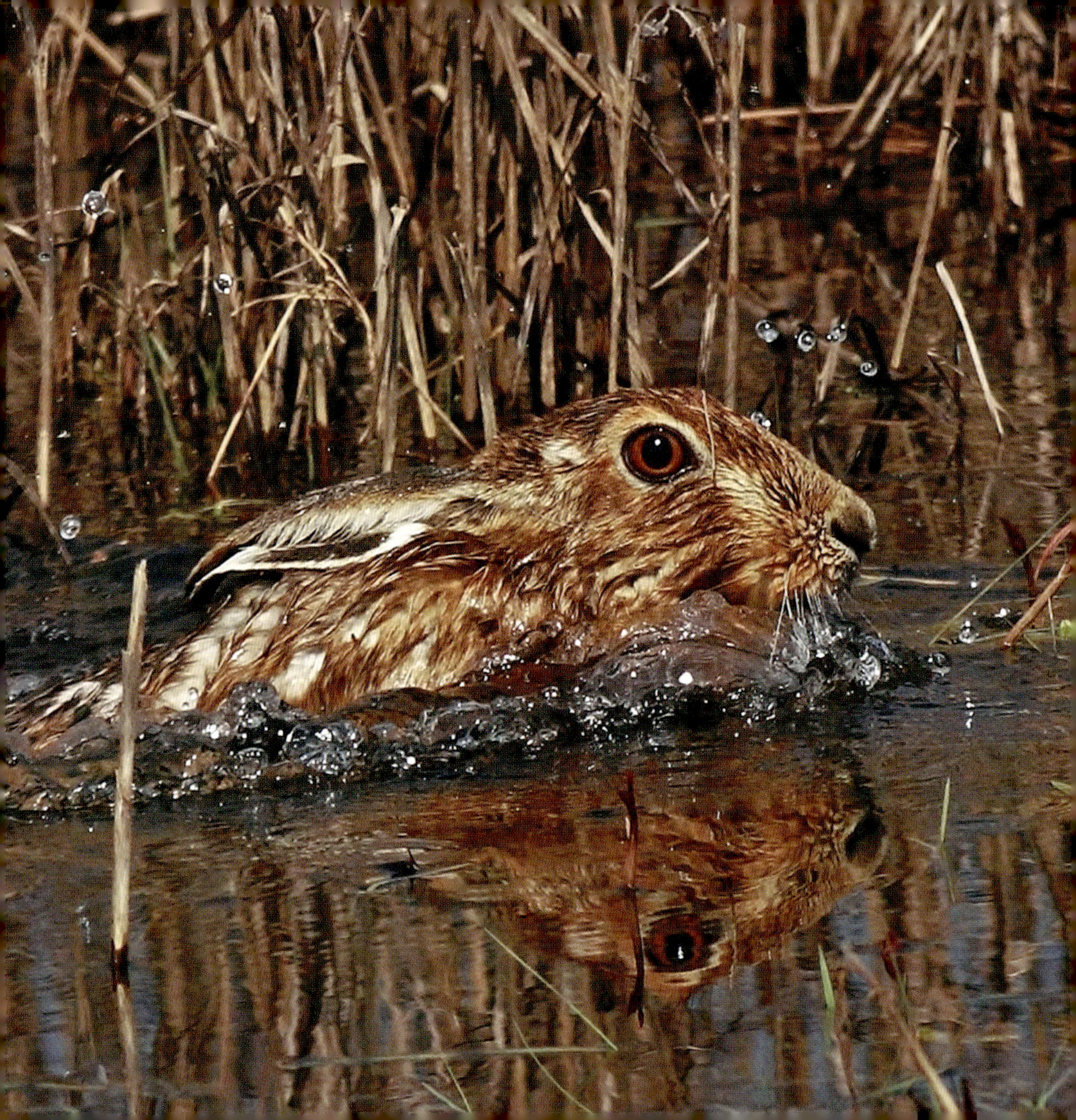

The brown hare is the only game species in England and Wales that does not have a close season.

Many game dealers sell hares to the public as well as wholesale and some export English hares to continental Europe (the Netherlands and France) and Ireland.

In most countries in Europe, hares are protected by a close season. This is the case in Austria, Belgium, Denmark, Finland, France, Germany, Greece, Hungary, Ireland, Italy, Luxembourg, the Netherlands, Poland, Slovenia, Spain, Sweden, and Switzerland. Scotland has recently implemented the Wildlife and Natural Environment (Scotland) Act 2011, introducing close seasons for the killing or taking of wild hares: for the brown hare, 1st February to 30th September; and for the mountain hare (*Lepus timidus*), 1st March to 31st July.

The brown hare is the only game species in England and Wales that does not have a close season. Organized shoots start in February, by which time the breeding period is underway so orphaned leverets, without maternal support, will almost certainly die of starvation as a result.

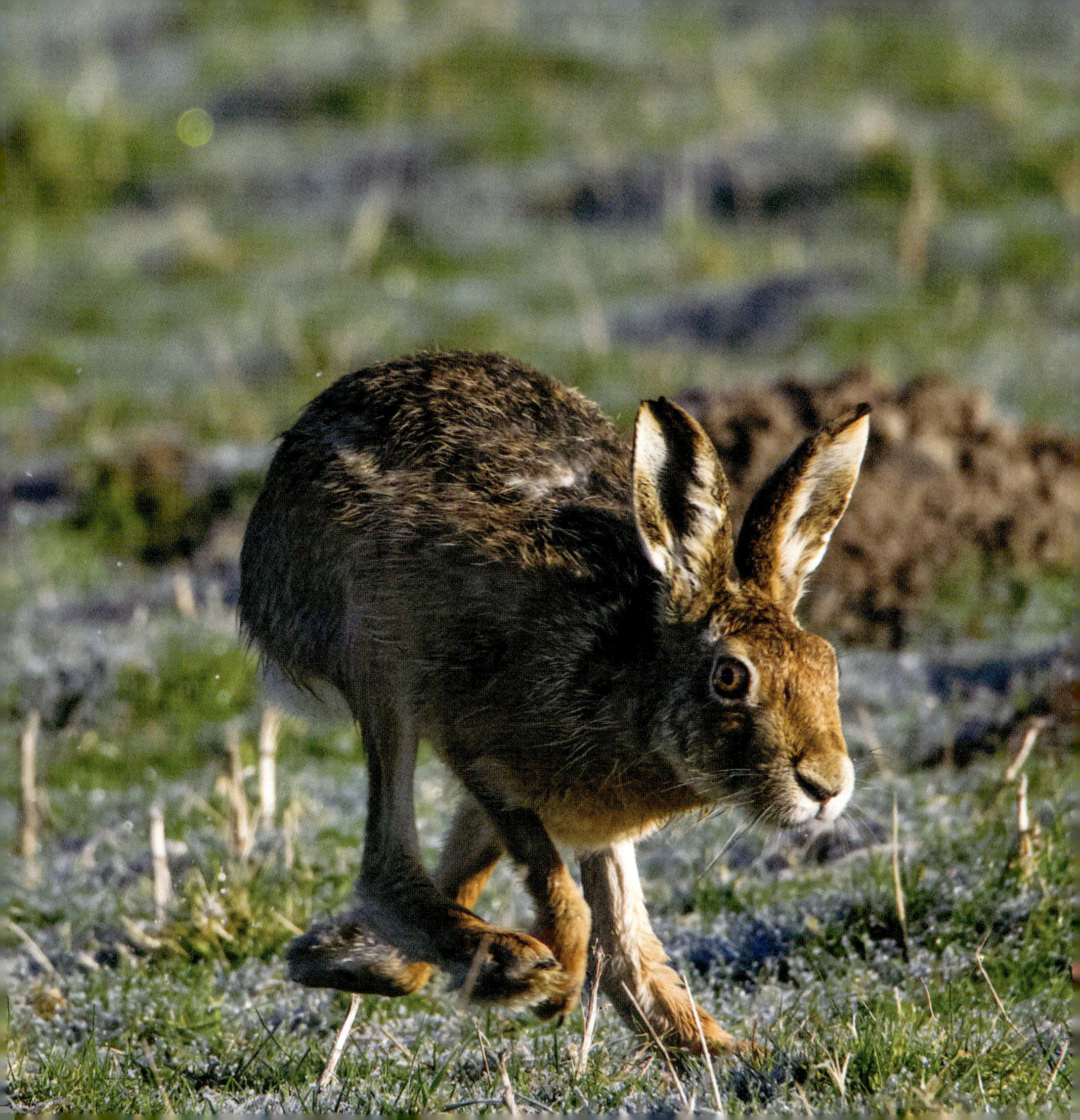

There are serious animal welfare implications of the systematic (and avoidable) losses of these young animals as a result of the loss of their lactating mothers by shooting. Over and above the loss of lactating females, many pregnant females are killed in February shoots. If we are to stop the decline of the brown hare in England and Wales, the need for a close season is self-evident.

Other threats to the hare population:

Disease. Hares are subject to a range of diseases that can cause mortality.

European Brown Hare Syndrome (EBHS). A virus related to the viral haemorrhagic disease of rabbits has been shown to cause EBHS. Outbreaks among European brown hares (*Lepus europaeus, Pallas*) of a fatal disease associated with severe liver damage have occurred in Sweden since the beginning of the 1980s. The disease EBHS, was recognised in Denmark in 1982 and was widespread in Denmark and southern Sweden by the early 1990s. Two species of hares are affected in Sweden, the European brown hare and the varying hare (*Lepus timidus, Linnaeus*). The disease is clearly seasonal, occurring most frequently in October, November and December.

EBHS is now in England. An HPT correspondent wrote about her personal experience of finding three dead hares lying in a running position and a fourth one died in her arms. She said, 'We had seen it staggering and clearly distressed and managed to corner it. It offered no resistance when I picked it up and I hoped to be able to take it to the RSPCA hospital at East Winch. Sadly this was not to be as it died in my arms within a few minutes. I was told that once they get to this stage, they have already had the disease for a while and death always follows.'

Coccidiosis. A protozoan infection of the intestine caused by parasites is common, usually later in the year when conditions are wet. It affects both the brown hare and the mountain hare and causes mild to moderate diarrhoea but can kill leverets especially in the autumn. (*Eimeria perforans* is the most predominant species affecting hares.)

Viral hemorrhagic disease is carried by vectors such as mosquitoes. This is especially lethal to pet rabbits but even hares will die of it, usually within hours, in which case there will be blood on the nose etc. A hare would not live long enough to get thin. Hares can also contract hepatitis, a liver disease.

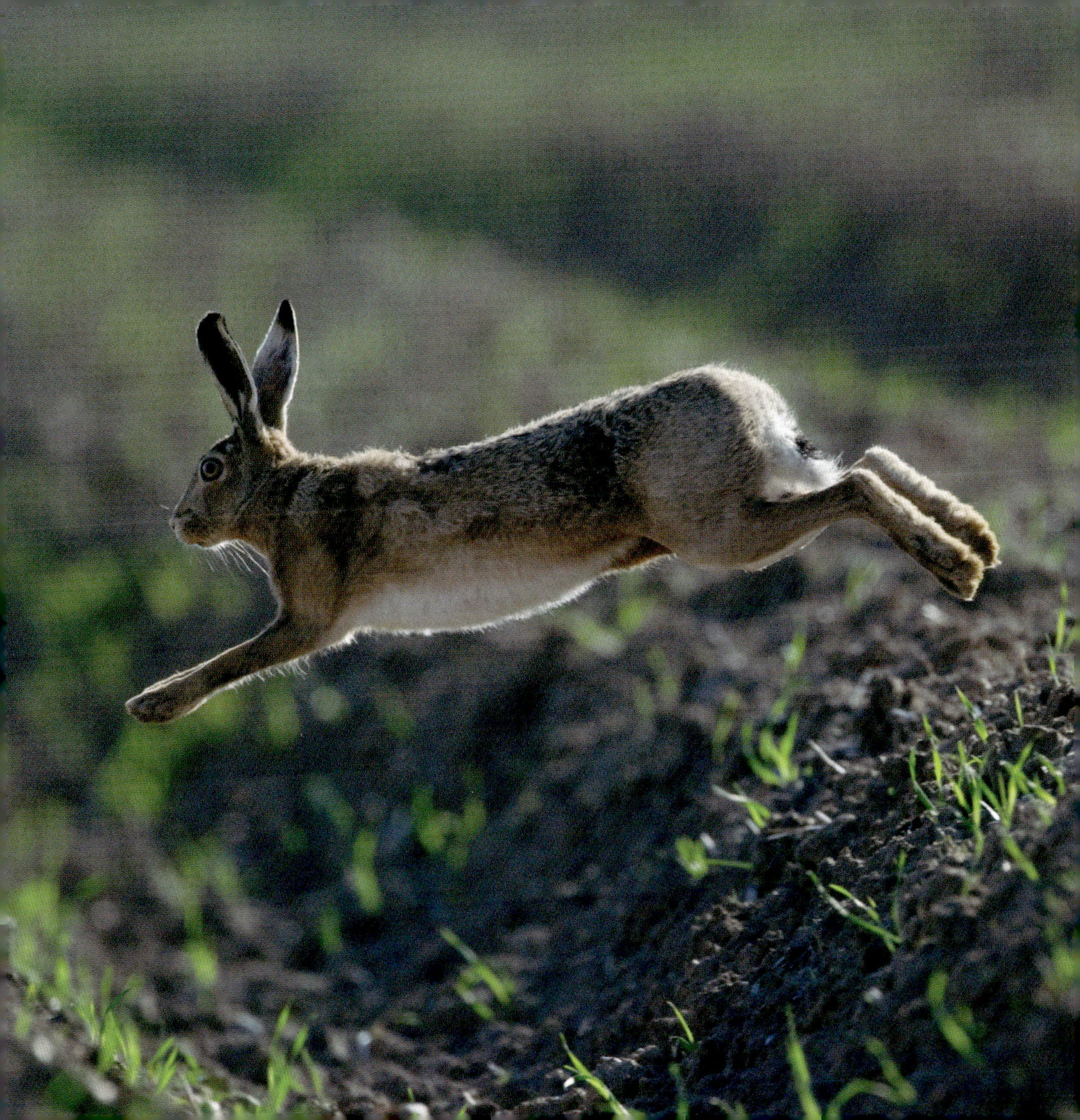

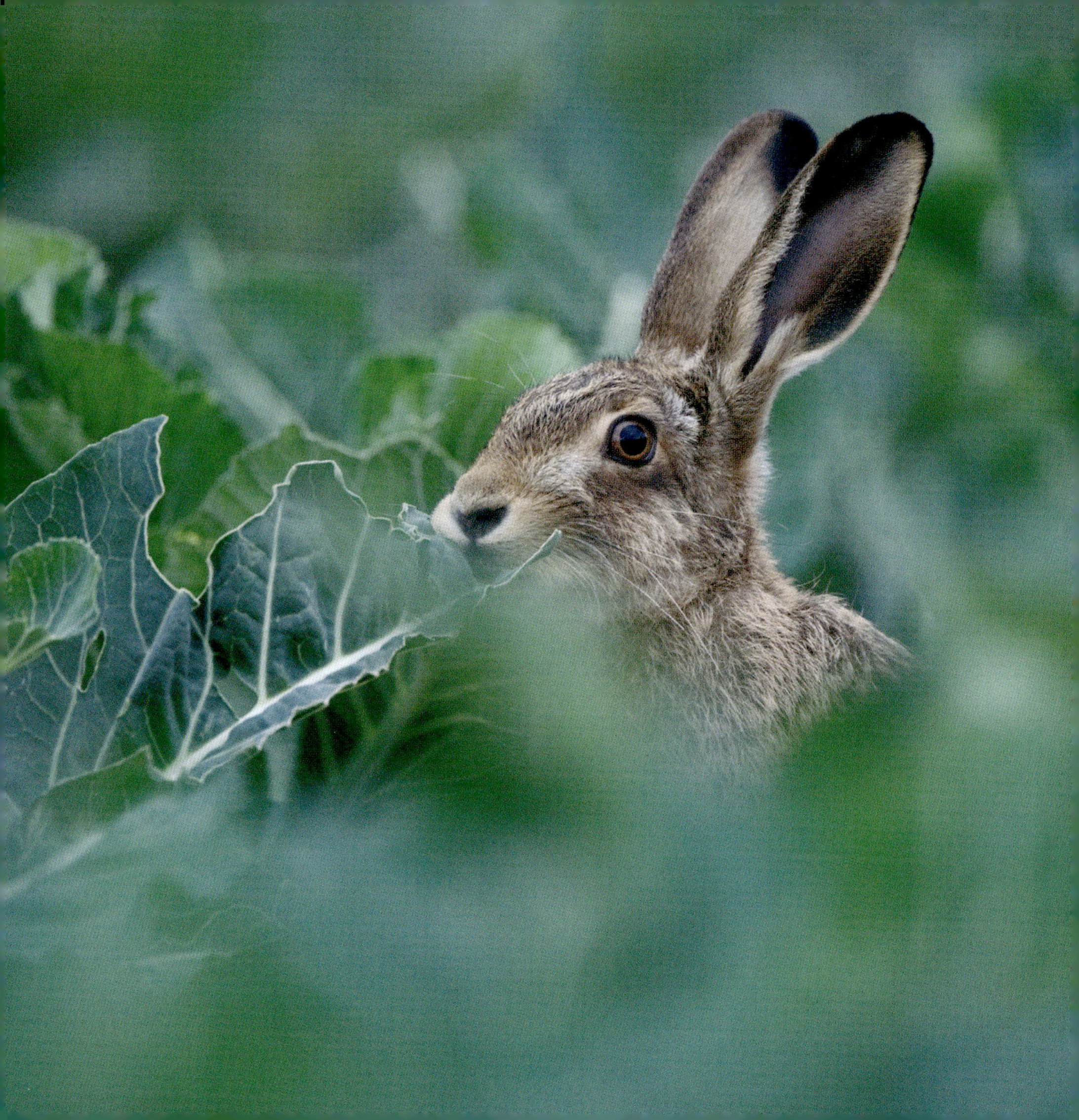

...and finally

Weed killer. In the past, when Paraquat was sprayed on fields to kill weeds, it unintentionally killed hares too as it got onto their feet and they licked it off, but this substance is now banned in England. RoundUp (glyphosate) is a quick-acting weed killer and would soon put the hares off eating any plants.

Also, it is unlikely to be used in winter when the hares are hungry and are therefore less likely to eat treated plants.

A serious threat to hare survival is adverse weather conditions. Excessive wet and cold weather, which we have seen in recent times, will take a heavy toll of the population. High leveret mortality is caused when their fur is continually wet and unable to dry out. A large number of hares, young and old, will have drowned in the floodwaters of 2013-14. Note that a report by Dr Toni Bunnell in 2011 for the Eden TV natural history channel listed the brown hare as one of the UK species most at risk of extinction by 2050.

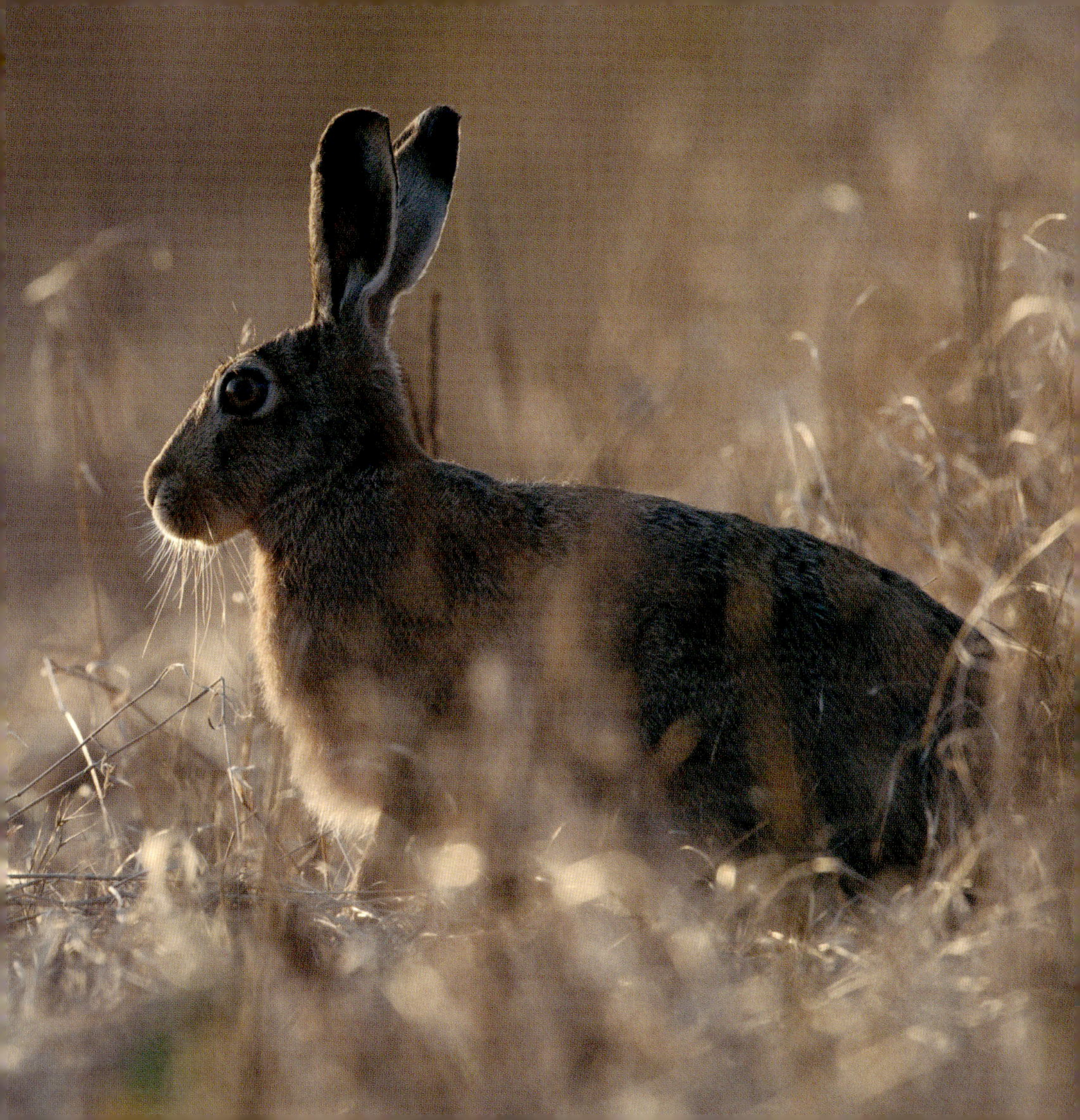

Hare encounters

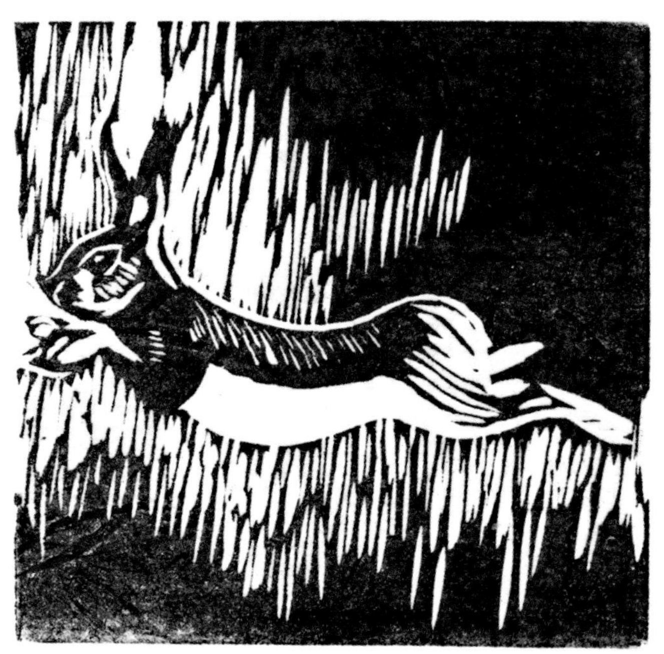

Face to face

"I was walking very early one morning in the lanes around my village, when I noticed something running down the centre of the road towards me. At first I thought it was a terrier-type dog but as it got closer I realised it was a hare. I was mesmerised and stood stock still. The wind was in the right direction (for me) and he/she got to within 10 feet of me before realising I was there. There are rhynes (ditches full of water) either side of the road and it was a long straight road so I also got to watch him/her run all the way back before going into a field. I felt like I'd had a magical encounter with a mystical creature and when I returned home looked for an organisation associated with hares. I found the HPT and joined."

Di, Somerset Levels

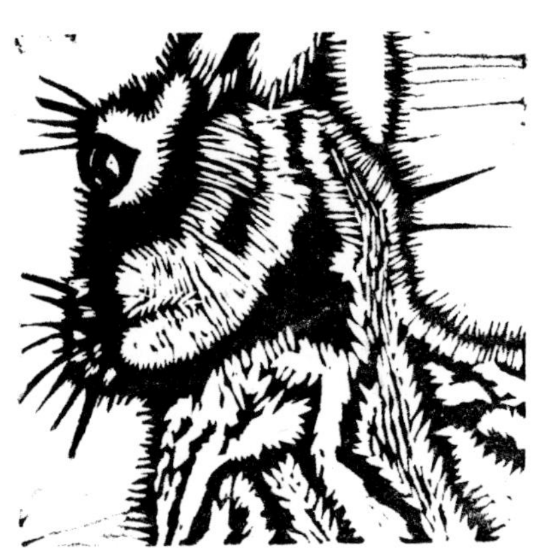

Close encounter

"I have been observing a population of hares near Pocklington in East Yorkshire almost daily, seeing up to fifteen in one field. One Sunday in June, I was standing astride my bike at the entrance to a field that had been drilled with grass seed (turf growing is prevalent in the Vale of York). There were four hares in the field and three loped off but one came over to me, I stood still and hardly dared breathe. He actually loped round me and my bike before going off along the side of the hedge but still unafraid. He was a juvenile, from his size, and I am guessing male from his boldness. Then he met a female (?) and they started boxing in the open before being joined by two more juveniles. Being able to see them so closely was amazing. When I speak of the hares, people say they have never seen one, or not for years, and I feel very privileged to see so many routinely."

HPT member Jackie

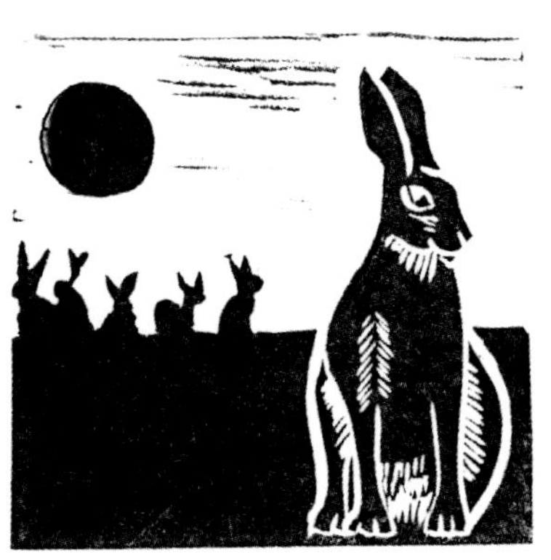

From birds to hares!

"I joined a local RSPB group and got into bird watching. Often, the trips out involved early starts and we would see hares quite often on these trips. It wasn't long before I felt more overjoyed at seeing the hares than the birds. Now, I do still go bird watching but hares are my main passion. I do feel privileged when I see them, especially now I've moved to the north-west where there just aren't as many hares around as where I used to live."

HPT member Linda

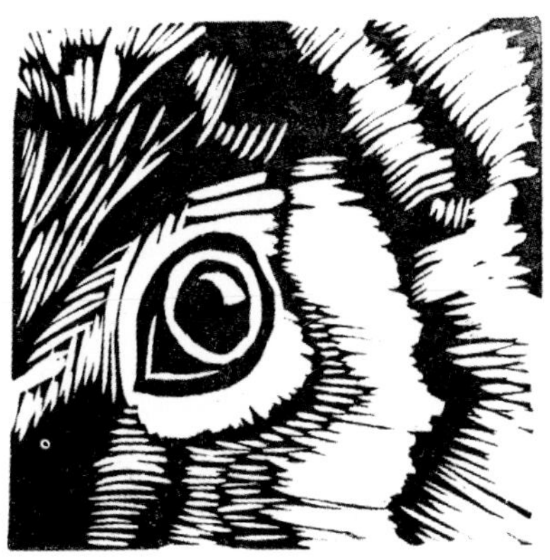

Sand baths

"We live on the edge of the Norfolk Marshes and have found a few things which help to bring the hares into our garden. After digging over a trench one summer in preparation for planting a new hedge, we found that the hares would come to roll in the sandy soil and lay in the trench for hours at a time. We then carefully sprayed off an area of grass near to the house to plant a wild flower patch and the same thing happened and, on some evenings, there would be four or five hares rolling and stretching out on the earth. Young leverets would come too and seemed to watch and copy the adults.

Having sowed the wildflowers and knowing that the bare earth would soon be covered, we left a fairly large bare area on the edge and dug this out a little deeper before filling it with play sand. During the summer the hares still come and get quite excited, leaping about and rolling in the warm sand. We assume they do this to keep the fleas and parasites at bay."

HPT members Tessa & Rob

Humbling experience

"Almost 35 years ago I was working in North Yorkshire looking after some ornamental woodlands. One day I was sitting in the woods having my lunch, when I noticed a hare about a dozen yards away that seemed to have appeared from nowhere. I decided to try the old country trick of sucking on my hand to make a squeaking noise to bring it closer and to my surprise it slowly came closer and closer. I was thinking that I had some kind of magic charm as it eventually came right up to me. I gently picked her up and she looked at me with the most beautiful hazel eyes... and died in my arms. It was such a magical experience

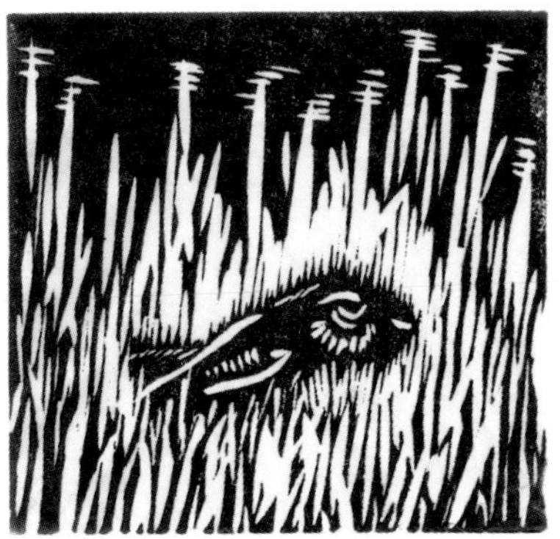

that I almost expected the hare to transform into a beautiful maiden! She was very light and as skinny as a rake and obviously had been at death's door, but I felt humbled by the experience."

Paul, Castle Howard North Yorkshire

A tasty morsel

"We also have two apple trees and hares love the windfall apples, many of which we gather up and put on the step outside our french doors and they soon get to know where to come for a treat and being very curious creatures sometimes peer in through the window! We have a bright halogen light on the back wall of our house and during the autumn/winter months we will put this on in the evenings and are able to watch the hares outside in the garden and on many occasions have seen leverets being fed. The hares don't seem bothered by the light at all – perhaps it just seems like moonlight to them.

There are many individual hares which we can recognise from their markings, behaviour, personalities and habits and it is such a privilege to live with these lovely, gentle creatures."

HPT members Tessa & Rob

Night time encounter

"My husband and I saw our first hare one night in Devon when we were driving down a single track country lane to the pub for dinner. We were going very slowly as it was so narrow and steep and suddenly there was this huge hare in the road in front of us. It lolloped slowly down the road in our headlights and then turned into a field. We were amazed by i) how big it was (nothing prepares you for that, it SO wasn't a rabbit) and ii) how very unconcerned it was by being followed by the car. I've seen other hares since but that night time encounter grabbed my heart."

HPT member Jane

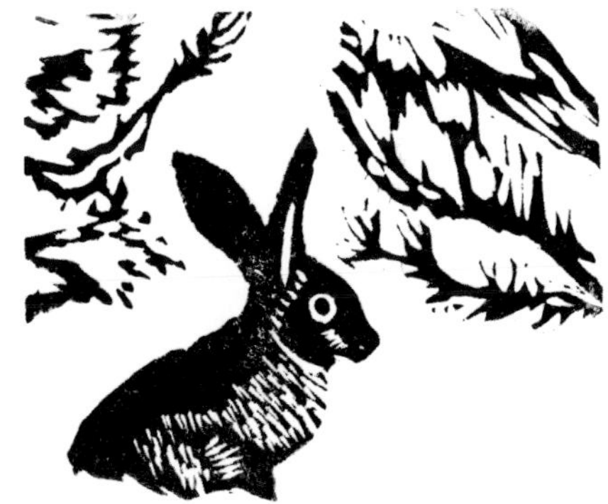

Encouraging hares

"We also leave several circles of uncut grass in the lawn about 6' diameter every spring and have had regular leveret births in these areas. Not all have survived, as stoats and crows are their main predators here. The hares love to come and feed on the flowering heads during the early summer. We cut these areas down to about 6" in the autumn as they don't seem to like the grass if it's too old. We have also had leveret births out in the open short grass and these babies have to make their own way to cover in the long grass or under a plant in the border. Hares like to sit with their backs to something so tree trunks, large logs or stones placed around the garden will help. Sometimes they will sit in this one place for the whole day and are very tolerant of us watching from the windows and taking photos. All the better if you can position these on an area of bare earth."

HPT members Tessa & Rob

Summer Solstice

"5am; Brown hares near Matlock, Peak district. Misty, cold, sunny.

Approximately twenty hares together. Pretty isolated, no houses for a few miles just the odd farm. Three ladies who were totally thrilled, and enthralled at seeing this wonderful sight over the wall. I have lived in the country all my life and am used to seeing hares in the area but never seen so many together. Magic!"

Summer Solstice 2014

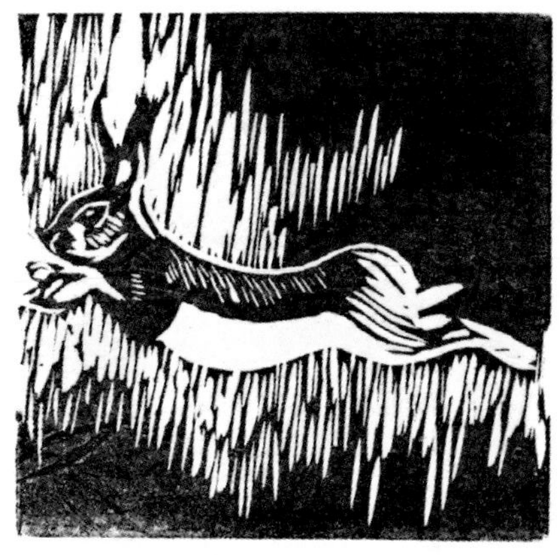

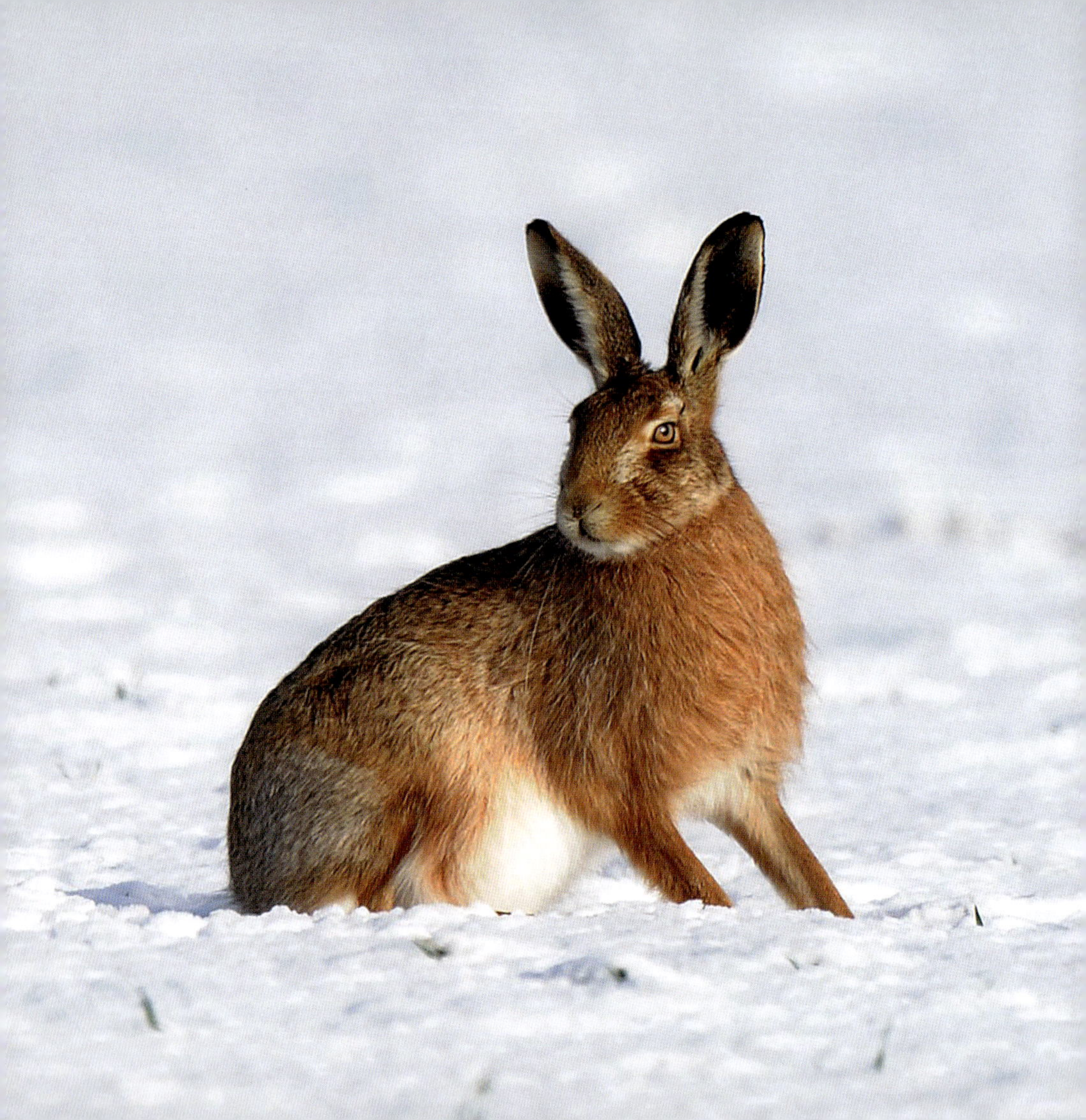

The hare in myth
and legend

The hare in myth and legend

The hare appears in many traditions and cultures as the image that represents the female, the lunar cycle, rebirth, fertility and longevity. The very nature of the animal itself seems to be embodied in the shape-shifting, ethereal representations; one moment representing sexuality, the next purity, foolishness and artful intelligence, as well as the feminine and the androgynous. It can be viewed as either the 'god/goddess' herself or merely a messenger moving through the moonlight from our world to that mysterious world beyond.

There are no actual records of brown hares in the British Isles before the Romans came.

However, Queen Boudica of the Iceni in AD61, is documented as either reading its entrails or setting one free before battle (depending on which source you believe) so it would appear that hares settled in quickly.

The Anglo-Saxons revered the hare and considered them lucky (hence the lucky rabbit's foot?) because of their connection with the goddess Ostara. Ostara, or Eostre, was the goddess of the moon and fertility, and a shape-shifter, the hare being the shape she took during the period of the full moon. It was Eostre who moved winter into spring and the Celtic/pagan festival of Ostara on 21st March, the spring equinox, always included the giving of eggs as a symbol of rebirth.

This festival of Ostara was turned into Easter by the encroaching Christians, and it would seem that superstitions to foster the feeling that hares should be feared were encouraged, (see fishermen's superstitions elsewhere in this book). In the Middle Ages, it was even believed that the hare could change its sex every other year. Hares began to be recognized, like black cats, as witch familiars or even in some legends as witches in animal form. Folk tales of all sorts began to include a passage where someone, often a lord/hunter but definitely a man would, during the hunt, follow a hare who would lead him into danger. Sometimes they ended well; the

Celtic warrior Oisin wounding a hare in the leg and following it into a thicket, found himself in an underground hall, before a beautiful woman sitting on a throne with a wounded leg... or not so well, the Dartmoor tale of the hunter Bowerman, who disturbed a coven and was lured by a revengeful young witch (in hare form) into a life-taking bog and turned by her into the stone formations now know as Hound Tor and Bowerman's Nose. Even these days it is still superstitiously believed that hares carry dead souls to their peace.

Agriculture too had myths about the hare. The last sheaf of reaped corn was sometimes call 'the hare' and its cutting, 'killing the hare', 'cutting the hare' or 'cutting the hare's tail off' had a full ritual: these ceremonies of the last sheaf are seen in France, Ireland and Germany and other parts of Europe.

Welsh mythology too is littered with stories about hares. Giraldus Cambrensis, in the 12th century, noted a belief that in order to suckle from a cow, a witch would turn into a hare.

Briefly, here is an outline of myths of note from around the world.

In Nordic legend, the hare was a holy animal special to Hulda (or Holda, Herke, Harfer) and a symbol of fertility. Holda's water sources, ponds and wells, will often use the word hare in their title and Holda's lights are traditionally carried by a group of hares.

We see a 'man in the moon' in European cultures but in Eastern societies there is a 'hare in the moon'. In China, the hare holds a pestle and mortar for the mixing of the elixir of immortality; furthermore he is the messenger of the deity of the moon and guards all wild animals. Folklore states that hares get pregnant by the touch of the moon, licking moonlight from a male hare's coat or crossing water by moonlight. In some areas of China the Moon Festival also features the hare, for its symbolic representation of fertility and female strength.

There is an Indian 'hare in the
moon' legend too. An early
incarnation of Buddha was a
hare. He was travelling with an
ape and a fox. A hungry beggar
(the god Indra in disguise) sent
each animal to find food. Only the
hare came back with nothing but,
not wanting to seem inhospitable,
jumped into the fire so that Indra
could gain sustenance. The hare
was rewarded by the god who
placed him as the 'hare in the
moon' for all eternity.

Hares were linked in Egyptian
myth to the cycles of the moon,
thought to be masculine when
waxing and feminine when
waning. It is not surprising
therefore that hares were
considered androgynous.

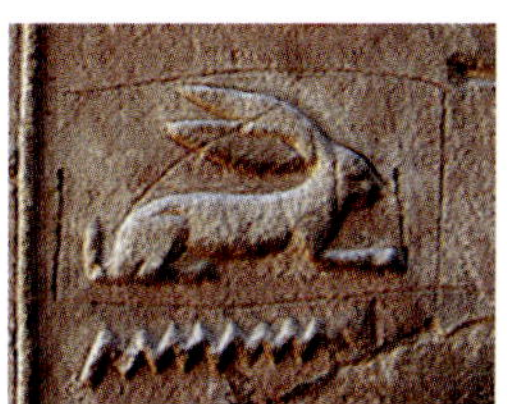

The temple at Dendera has a
hare-headed goddess (Unut or
Wenet) and god, possibly Osiris
(also Wepaut or Un-nefer).
Annually, Osiris was sacrificed to
the Nile in the form of a hare. The
Egyptian hieroglyph for 'to be' or
'to exist' is a hare on a wave.

Japanese legend has the hare
being created as the first animal
on earth and as a result he
becomes the messenger to the
gods, whilst they create the rest
of the animals in preparation for
the arrival of mankind.

The hare was the embodiment of romantic love in Greco-Roman mythology. As well as love this also encompassed lust, plenty and fruitfulness, and Pliny the

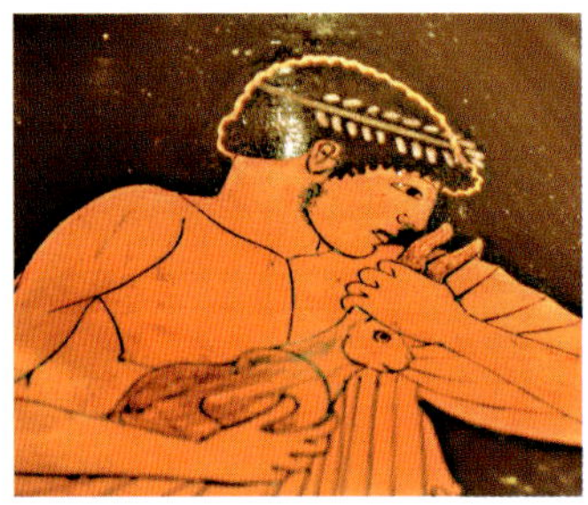

Elder recommended the meat as a cure for sterility and an aid to sexual attraction. They even played a part in homosexual love, as an older male lover might present his younger love with little gifts, like a hare or a bottle of oil or a toy.

In West Africa, many tribes perceive the hare as the inept trickster, a rascally clown. In one tale, the Moon sends Hare to tell mankind that, as the moon waxes and wanes, so shall humans have the gift of immortality. Hare gets the story wrong and mankind gets mortality instead. In a rage, the Moon beats Hare and splits his nose/lip... and so he looks today. Subsequently, as a penance, Hare is charged with leading the dead to the afterlife.

Amongst Native Americans too the hare is the trickster of the tale, particularly with the Algonquin-speaking peoples. It is considered probable that hare stories from Africa travelled to North America on the slaving

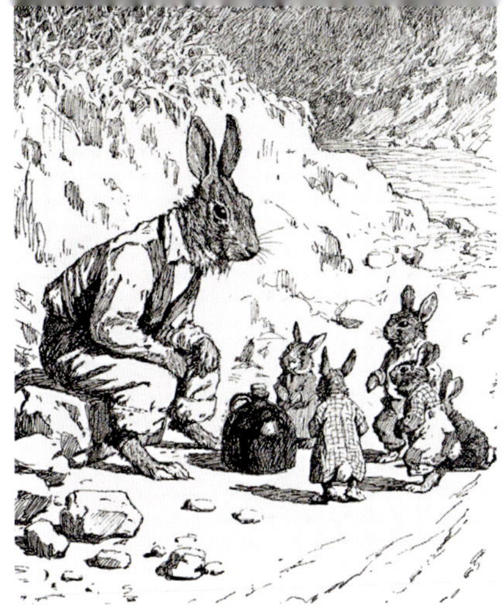

Image courtesy of The Wren's Nest Joel Chandler Harris museum Atlanta Georgia. Original illustration for the 1881 edition by AB Frost.

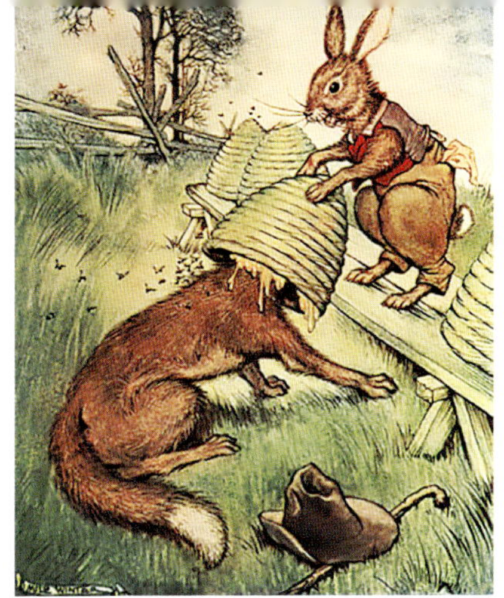

Image courtesy of The Project Gutenberg. Illustration by Milo Winter 1917.

ships and were then incorporated into tales with which tribes, such as the Cherokees, were already familiar. Eventually these stories became the fables of the famous/infamous Br'er Rabbit of the American South. Passed orally amongst the slaves, the poor down at heel Br'er (obviously a hare/jack rabbit from all the illustrations) was the embodiment of all their dreams as he, through his intelligence and quick wits, outdoes his stronger, richer opponents.

The Br'er Rabbit stories were finally published in the 19th century by Joel Chandler Harris and narrated by the fictional Uncle Remus.

Fishing communities superstitions

Fishing communities were well known for their strange hare superstitions.

Scotland

If the word 'hare', 'rabbit' or 'pig' was spoken on board then boats would be turned around or would not leave the harbour, and if a hare crossed your path on the way to your boat, that was the end of the day's fishing too. It was considered a very bad curse.

Wales

In the Rhondda, however, there was a proverb, 'A witch in the morning, success in the afternoon', meaning a hare crossing your path in the morning would bring good luck in the afternoon.

The hare has several names in Welsh, *cath-y-coed*, the cat of the wood or *cath-hirdaith*, the cat who makes a long journey.

Ireland

If fishermen on their way to the water met a woman (still worse if she happened to be red-haired or barefoot), they knew instinctively that they would catch nothing that day, and generally returned home. It was similarly regarded as unlucky to meet a hare, a rabbit, a priest, or a fox.

England

Near a Cornish seaport, if you saw a white hare that would mean that a storm was coming.

The many names of the hare

the stag of the cabbages

the stag of the stubble

the furze cat

the friendless one

the cat of the wood

the fast-traveller

the jumper

the swift-as-wind

the dew-hopper

the light-foot

the white-bellied one

the animal that no one dares to name

the slink-away

Old Big-bum

the fidgety-footed one

Saint Anselm

According to Eadmer's 'Life of St. Anselm', in 1097 Saint Anselm, who was then Archbishop of Canterbury, was riding out with the young men and dogs of his household when they put up a hare. The frightened animal ran to seek refuge between the legs of the Saint's horse and he reined it in to ensure safe sanctuary for the hare.

Eadmer who was a monk himself claims to have been there when this happened. He explains how Anselm, after calling off the dogs and forbidding them to give chase and thus ensuring that the hare could escape, burst into tears when members of the group laughed at the predicament of the hare. Anselm likened the poor hare to the plight of the human soul after death, surrounded by laughing and jeering demons, and longing for support and protection and a kindly hand to be held out to defend him. Although Eadmer does not stress the 'miraculous' nature of the tale, the moral to any listener, particularly in the Middle Ages, would have been clear.

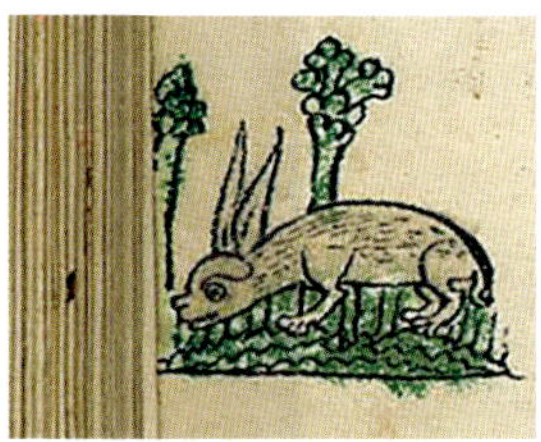

This little hare has been added at some point to the manuscript of St Anselm's Similitudes, possibly to illustrate this tale.

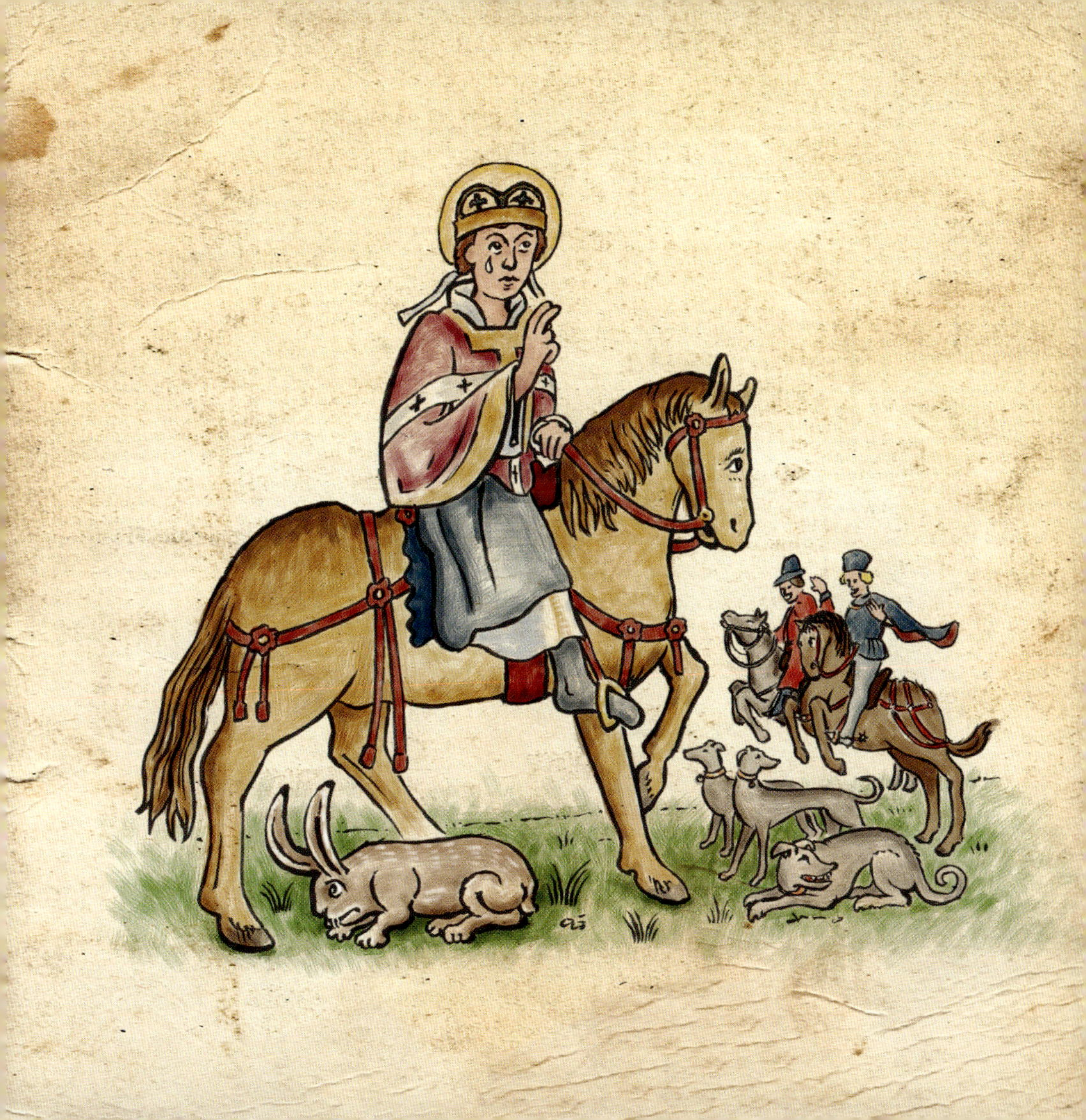

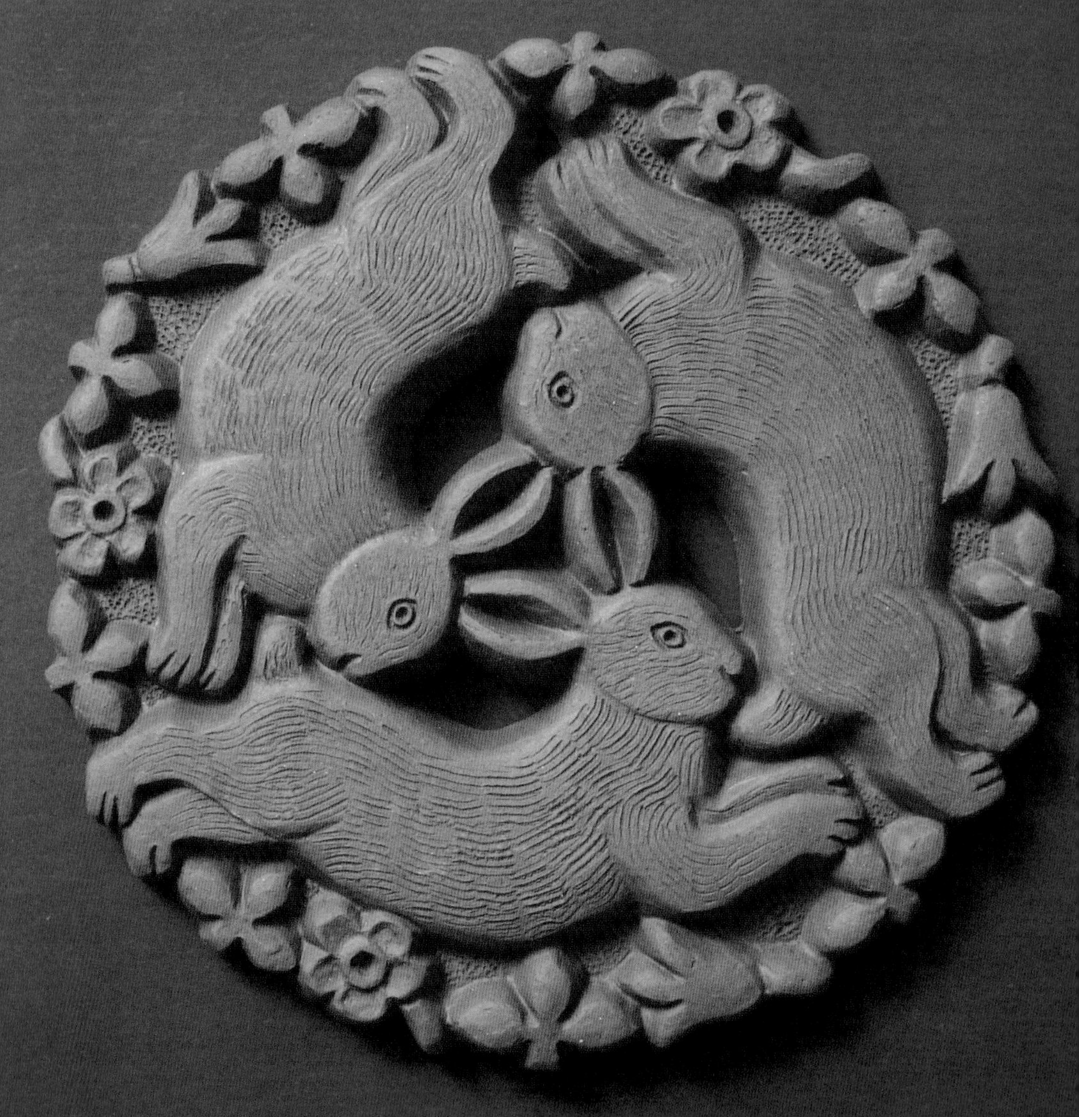

The Triskele hares

The Triskele hares symbol is very ancient and has been found across the world in Islamic, Buddhist and even Jewish depictions as well as Celtic and Christian myth and legend.

Three hares are depicted running in a circle and joined by their ears, which form a triangle. Each hare appears to have two ears but actually there are only three ears shown in the centre of the design. An ancient depiction from the 16th century in Paderborn Cathedral, Germany comes with a little poem, which translates as:

The hares and ears are three. And yet each hare has two (you see).

The hare, as we know, has been symbolically linked through thousands of years with the moon, fertility and the Goddess of nature. Its solitary behaviour, together with its nocturnal habits and speed, have made it a creature of mystery and magic. Surprisingly perhaps, there seems to be no documented record of what the symbol actually means. It was believed in ancient times that the hare was an hermaphrodite and therefore could bear young whilst still a virgin. This, linked to the 'threeness' of the image, may explain its use in churches and a possible association with the Virgin Mary and the Trinity.

Left: Three Hares by Black Dog of Wells

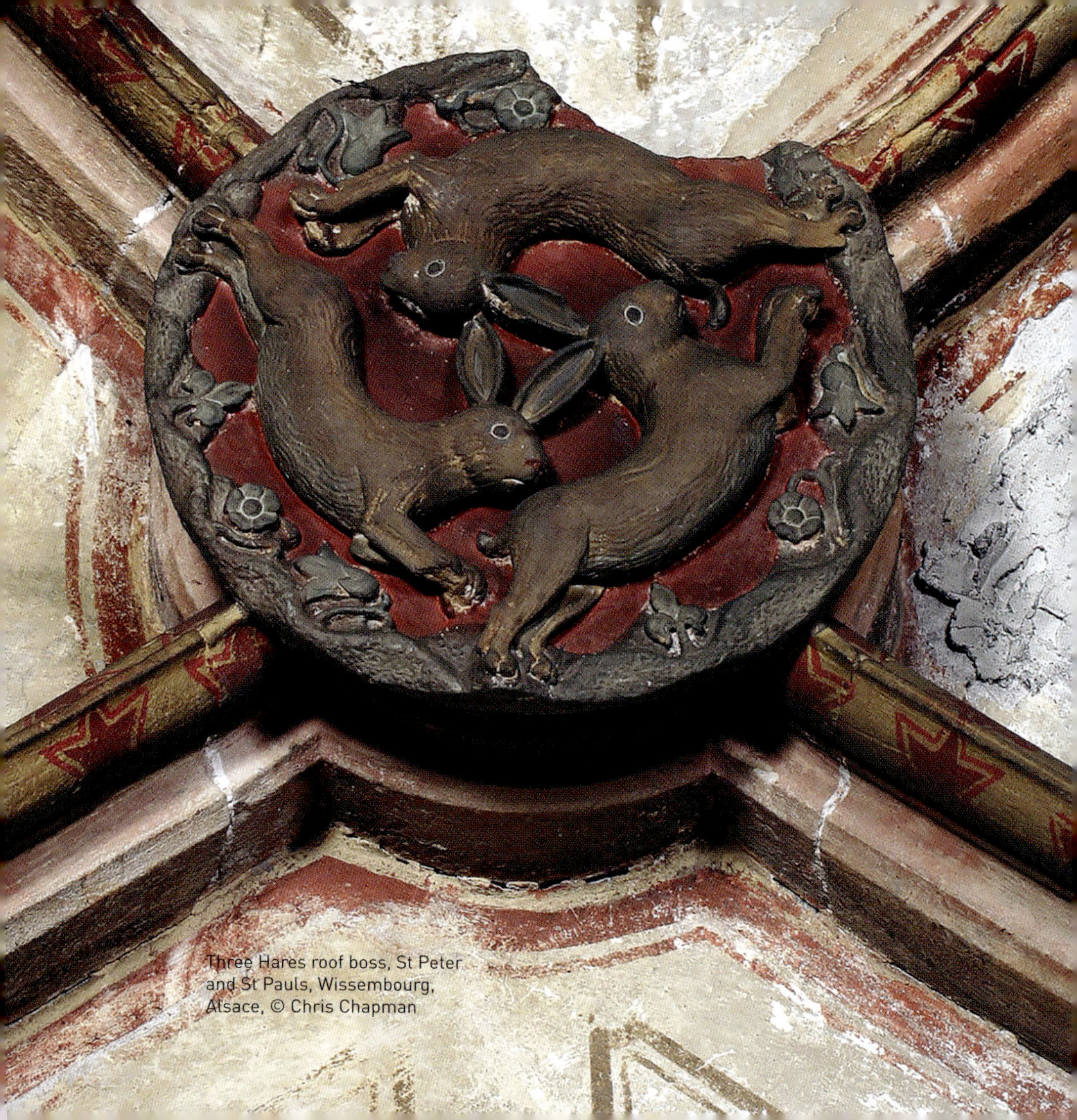

Three Hares roof boss, St Peter
and St Pauls, Wissembourg,
Alsace, © Chris Chapman

It is often found that carvings and decorations in churches, particularly very ancient ones, are a mix of pre-Christian and Christian imagery and to the congregation there would seem to be no conflict between the use of a green man or a triskele hare symbol with those of the cross or the saints.

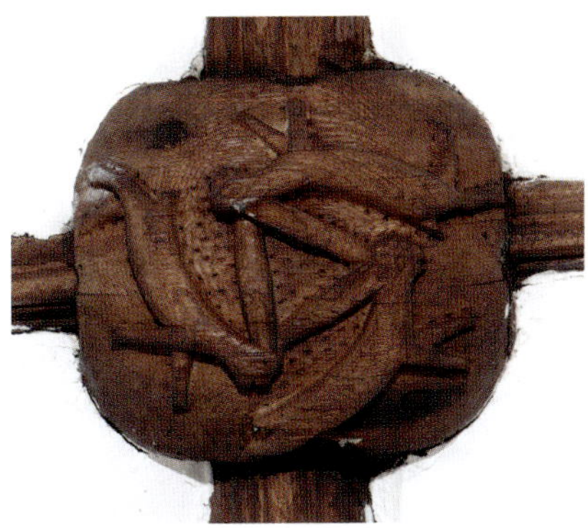

Three Hares roof boss, Cheriton Bishop, Devon © Chris Chapman

The first known examples are to be found in the Buddhist cave temples near Dunhuang, China, dating from 581-907 AD. It is thought that the three hares design was carried along the Silk Road during the 13th and 14th centuries, when trading from east to west was safely established for the first time. It is easy to think of traders bringing silks and reliquaries wrapped in fabrics bearing an interesting and new motif, causing a stir when they reached their destination in some church or cathedral in Europe or England. The fabrics would have made vestments and shrine dressings and would no doubt have made medieval craftsman look to their representational skills.

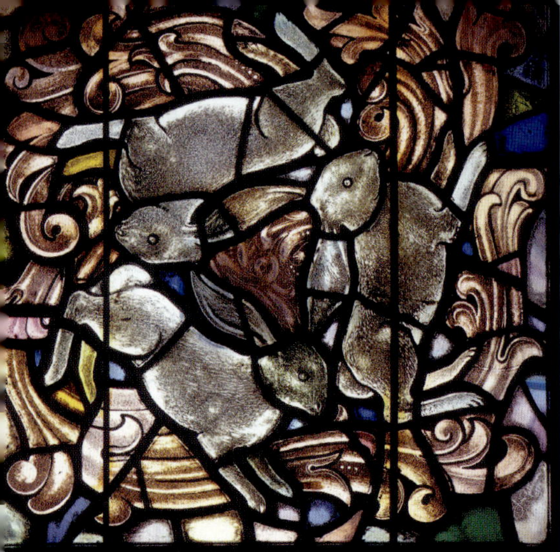

The Three Hares, Castle Inn, Lydford, Devon
© Chris Chapman

Once set loose and over time in the decorative world of the West, the image can be found in places as disparate as the plaster ceiling of a farmhouse and a stained glass window in a pub (both in Devon).

'A Survey of the Cathedral of St. David' published in 1717 by Browne Willis seems to be the first literary reference to the three hares. The painted stone boss is in the Lady Chapel in the cathedral in Pembrokeshire.

In Britain, roof bosses bearing the motif can most commonly be found in Devon, where there are an astonishing seventeen parish churches with the image. The cultural environmentalist, Dr. Tom Greeves, who comes from Tavistock, has been documenting and studying the three hares in all its manifestations since the 1980s. In 2000, with the art researcher Sue Andrew and the Devon documentary photographer Chris Chapman, he formed The Three Hares Project, with the aim of researching and recording all known occurrences.

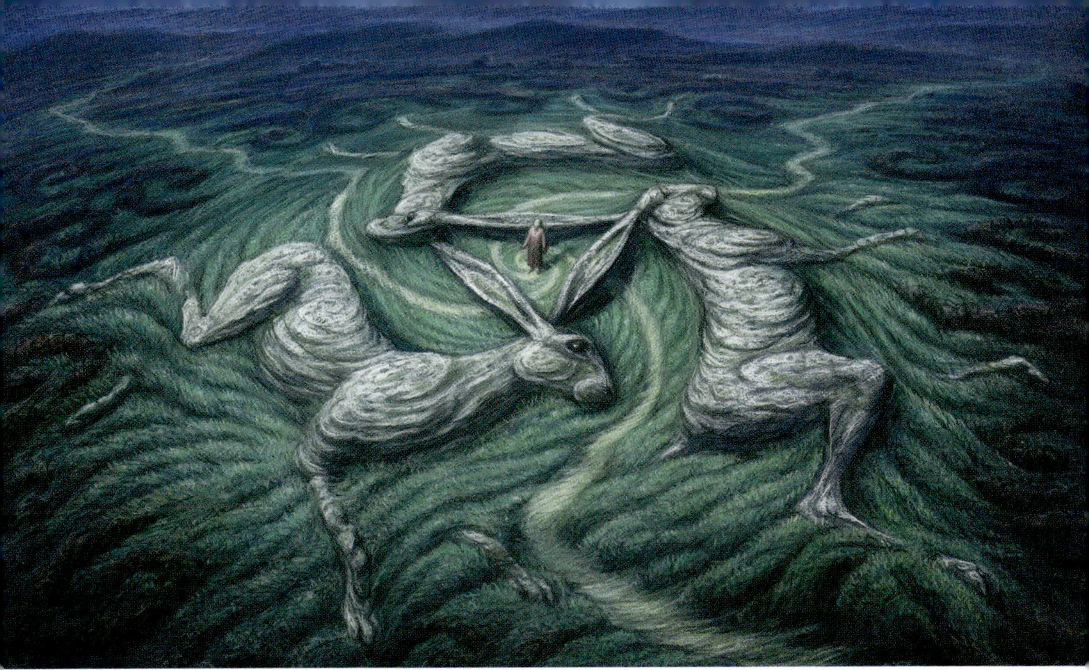

Three Hares Tor by Virginia Lee www.virginialee.co.uk

New examples are coming to light all the time. For more detailed information, go to their fascinating website at www. chrischapmanphotography.co.uk and click on the Three Hares Project.

The triskele hares have been inspiring artists for centuries and this modern interpretation by the painter Virginia Lee from Devon seems to capture the all-encompassing nature of the image.

St Melangell

In Ireland, around AD 590, St Melangell, who was of royal birth, wanted to lead a religious rather than a royal life. However, she was expected by her father King Jowchel to make a good marriage. Consequently, she fled from Ireland across the Irish Sea to Wales. The place she chose to settle was Pennant, an isolated but beautiful spot at the head of the Tanat Valley in North Wales. There, probably with the help of at least one servant or friend, she devoted herself to God; a cave became her cell and she lived there as a hermit for at least a decade.

Her legend has been translated from a 17th century manuscript by Professor Oliver Davies of St. David's College, Lampeter, and tells a tale of determination and love.

It happened that in AD 604 Prince Brychwel (Brochwel) Ysgithrog of Pengwern, Powys was out hunting, when his hounds put up a hare. Eventually, the hare dived into a dense bramble thicket and sitting in a clearing within it, praying, was St Melangell. The hare sheltered safely within the folds of her clothes. The hounds would not enter the clearing and Melangell would not give up the hare. Prince Brychwel had never been denied before and he requested an explanation from her.

After she had told of her life, the Prince was so moved by her devotion to God and strength of character that he said, *'O most worthy Melangell, I perceive that thou art the handmaiden of the true God. Because it hath pleased Him for thy merits to give protection to this little wild hare from the attack and pursuit of the ravening hounds, I give and present to thee with willing mind these my lands for the service of God, to be a perpetual asylum and refuge. If any men or women flee hither to seek thy protection, provided they do not pollute thy sanctuary, let no prince or chieftain be so rash towards God as to attempt to drag them forth'.*

As a consequence of his most

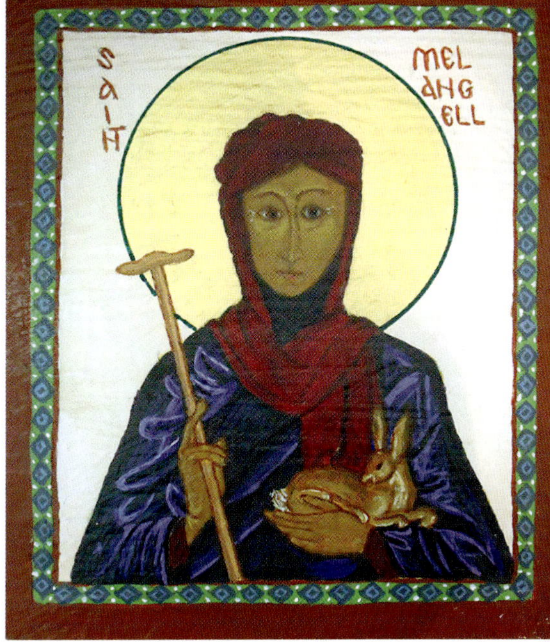

generous gift (his heirs, in perpetuity, continued to honour his bequest), the Pennant Melangell as it became known, became and remains a sanctuary for those devoted to God. Melangell lived on there for more than 35 years and gradually other women came to join her in her monastic life of prayer and good works. Hares continued to be much loved by her and were even known locally as Wyn Melangell (St Melangell's lambs). Even in present times, the local hunters of Cwm Pennant will not kill hares.

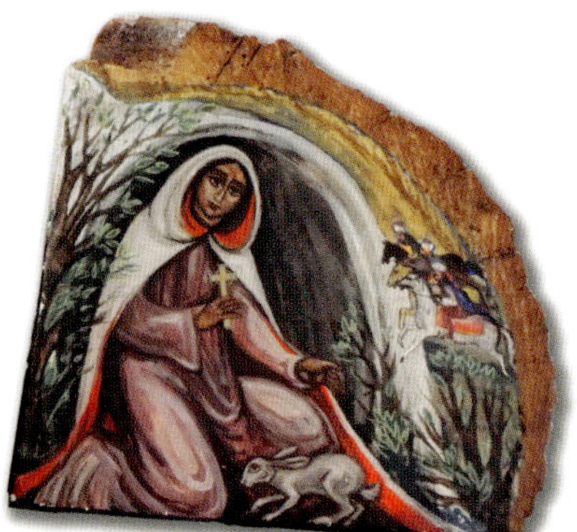

St Melangell is known in Latin as Monacella.

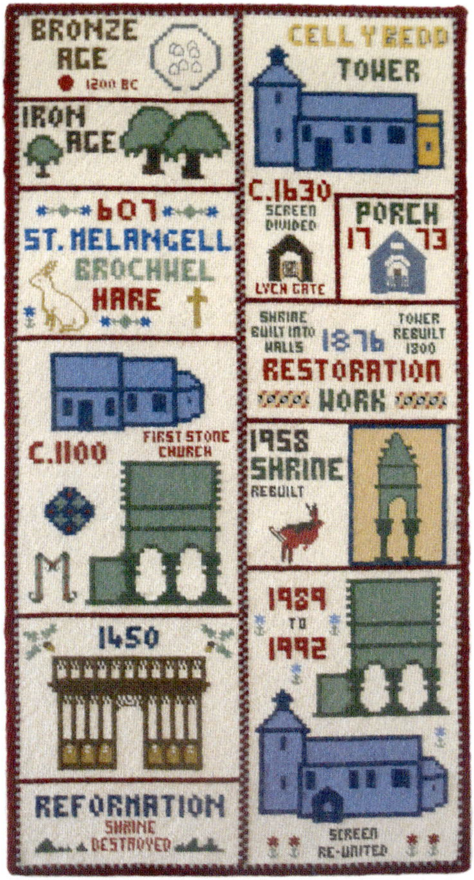

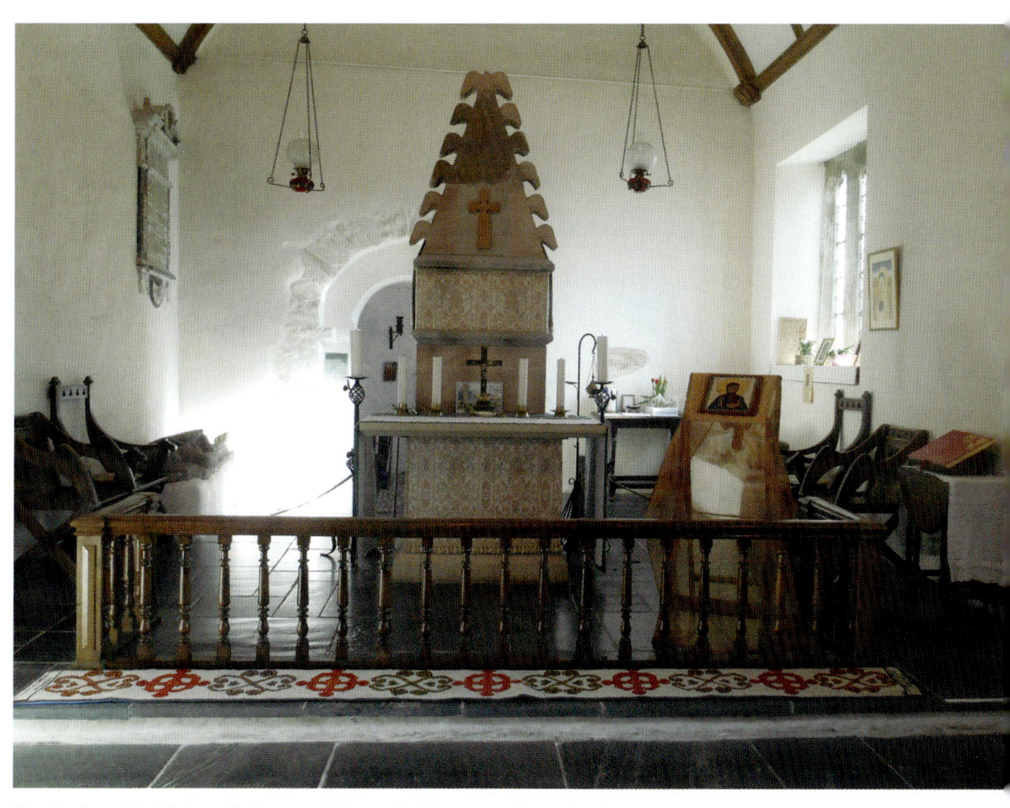

The Shrine of St. Melangell, Pennant Melangell, Llangynog, Powys, Wales

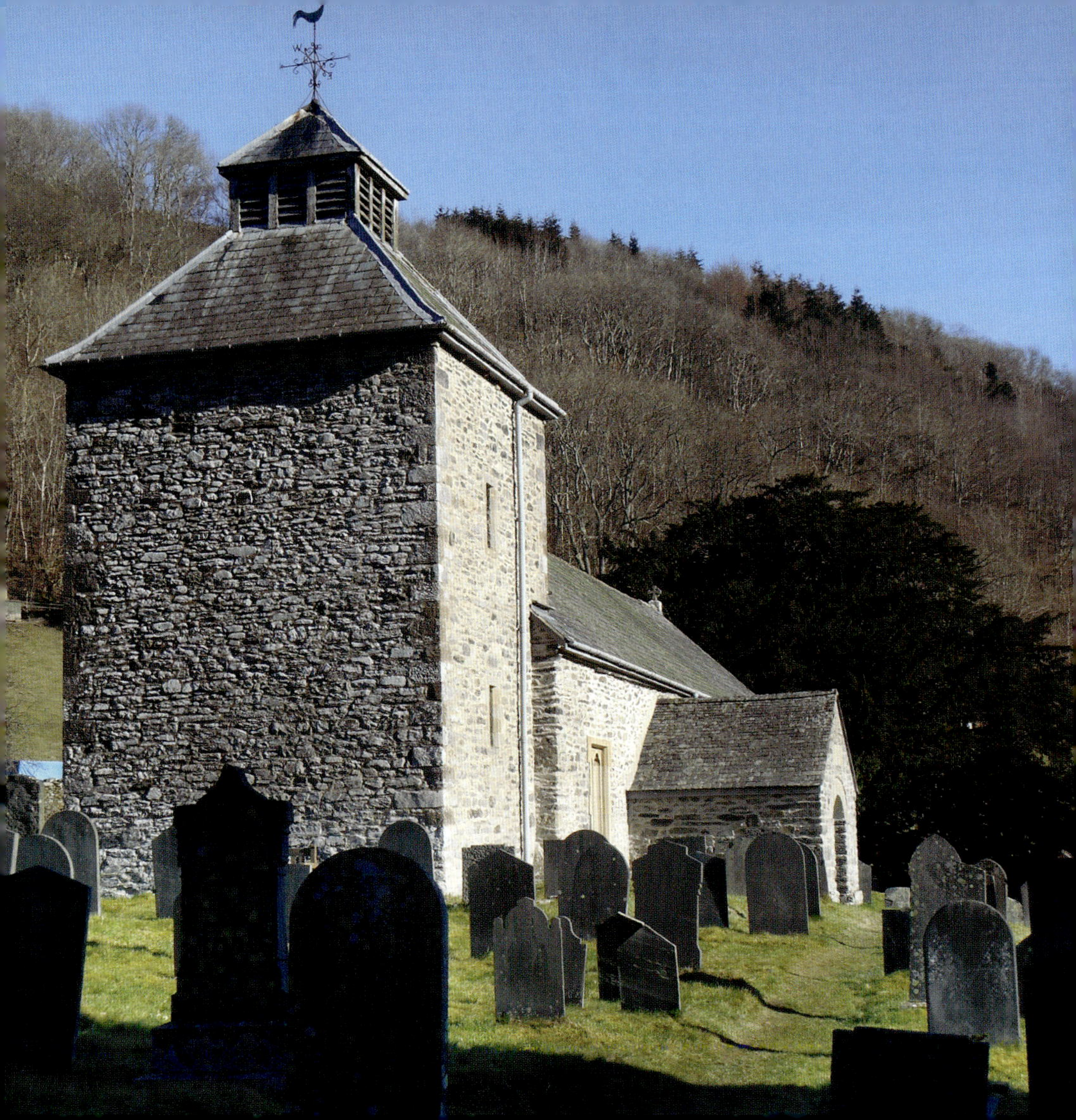

St Melangell's Church

There has been a Christian church on the site for over 1200 years – it is now a Grade I listed building. It nestles at the base of the Berwyn Mountains, quiet and serene. Unusually, the church sits within a circular Bronze Age site with some yew trees believed to be two thousand years old. The earliest parts of the building date from the 12th century and the most recent from 1990 when the apse was rebuilt on its original foundations.

Inside the church there is a 15th century rood screen made of oak, depicting the story of the saint and Prince Brychwel, as well as the usual collection of church accoutrement from a variety of subsequent periods.

The most interesting piece, however, is the 12th century shrine to St Melangell. Its history alone makes it a thing of note as it was dismantled after the Reformation to save it from destruction, and the stones with their interesting carvings were built into the walls of the church and the lych-gate to effectively 'hide' them. During the 20th century, they were reconstituted into the large and impressive shrine we see in the church today. The church was found to be in very poor repair at the end of the 1980s but, following a full scale restoration finally completed in 1992, it has become a focal point for pilgrims and soul seekers from the British Isles and beyond.

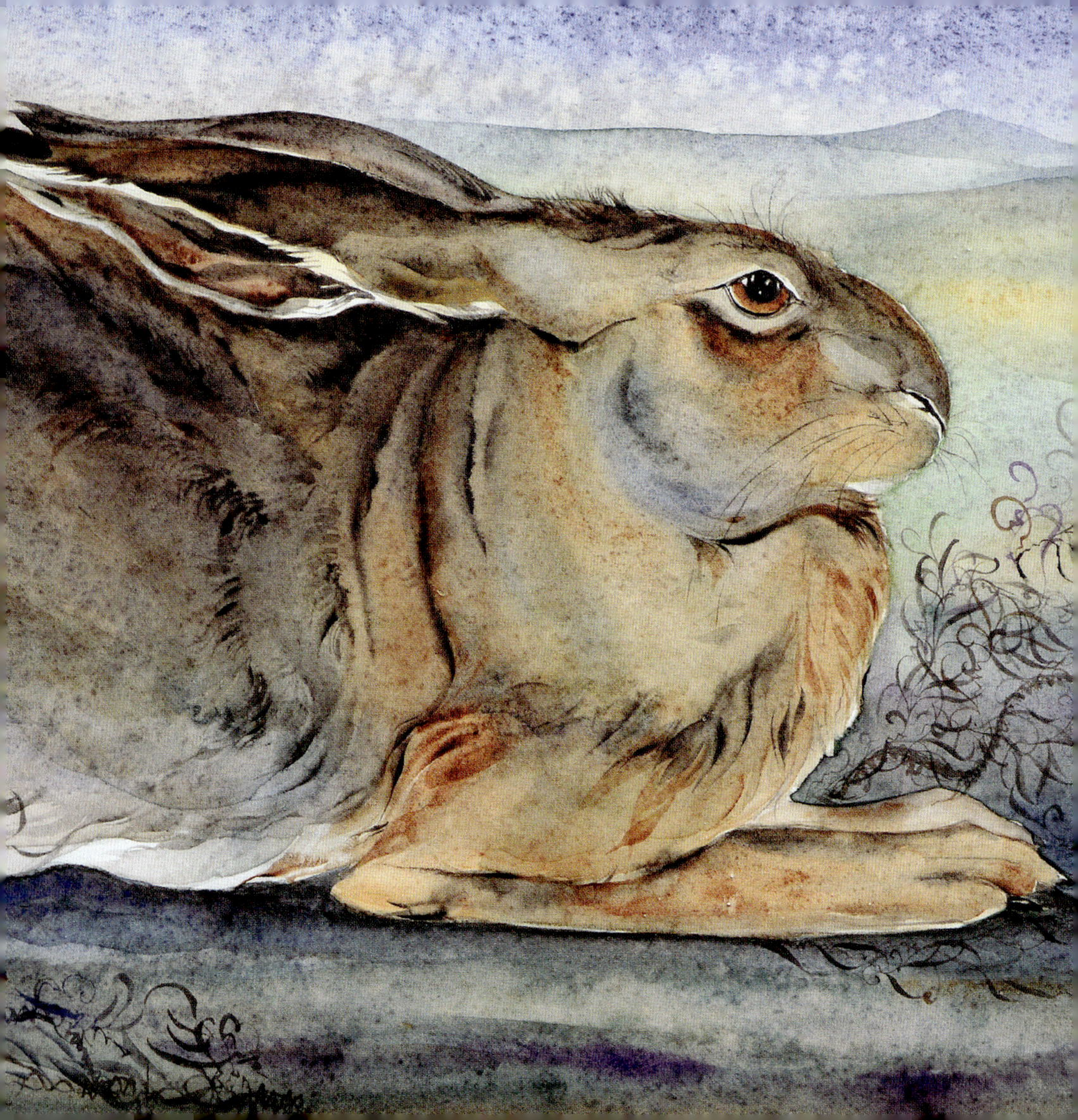

The Old Hare in Spring: 1502
by Jackie Morris

The warm spring sunlight traps in my fur as I sit at the field's edge crouched, low to the earth, remembering.

They had thought to punish me, as they turned my skin to fur, bent my bones and back, made my eyes two dark globes of amber, ears stretched and fine. What they saw as a punishment I perceived as a blessing.

Woodcat they made me. Woman I was born.

At first, afterwards, I remained close to the village, afeared of the wild things, drawn back to my own kind, watchful, hidden. Familiar scent of woodsmoke drew me in like a magnet. As time moved on, so did I. All that was human in me began to fall away. My fear of the wild turned to love, of wild places, dark spaces. I moved out across the land and became a pilgrim creature of dusk and of dawn. I dwelt in the twilight hours when the owl owned the sky. By night I sheltered in scrapes and hollows, protected by trees. Sometimes in the heat of summer I would stretch out in the sunshine, long in the meadow flowers.

The wild hares accepted me as humans never had. I lived among lapwings, curlew and crow, knowing no borders. As a girl I had thought that the wild hares laid eggs and now I understood why I thought that. Each year in spring I would dance with the

wild hares, mate and lay my
children in soft scoops of earth.
Stone still they would sit, alone,
while I watched from a distance.
All around them the children of
birds would hatch from delicate
eggs. We shared watch over our
young, my ears sharp for sound,
their eyes, lifted high on wings,
my nose, all aware of the shape
and the scent of weasel, cat and
fox, the shadow of the eagle, the
stoop of the hawk.

Some children I lost, many I
raised, always I wandered.

Then one day, at a time when the
corn was high, beautiful cover
hiding us all from predators' eyes,
people came to cut it down, with
curved knives, to bind it in stooks.
They left a corner, the hare's

corner, and here we all gathered
to wait for them to leave. But
next came the men with their
hounds and their hawks. The
hounds came in first and chased
us all out and we ran across the
stubble field, zigzagged through
the corn stooks, leaping over
hedges. Many were killed, some
escaped. I was tumbled by dogs
and lay as if dead, but somehow
remained hidden at the field's
edge, forgotten by the hunters.

All night pain and hunger
and thirst were my terrible
companions until sleep pulled me
closer to death.

I woke to the sound of children's
voices. Small hands reached
down to cradle my broken body,
my slow moth breath so shallow.

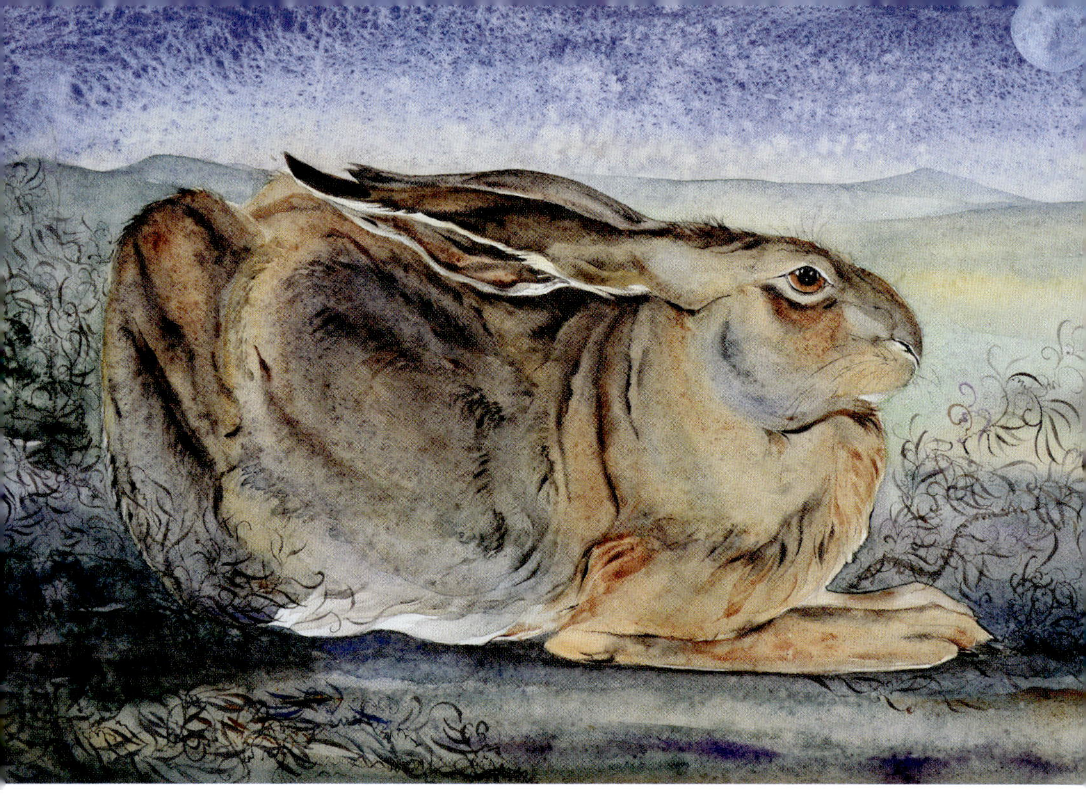

They carried me, gentle as a baby,
over the fields and into the town,
to him. And he nursed me, back
to health, mended my broken
bones, brought me
sweet grasses.

Never had anyone looked at
me as he did, not when I was a
woman, never when I became a
hare. I sat, still as stones, hare-
quiet, patient. Calm. That is how
he made me feel. Calm. He drew

me. Then he painted. Each mark
he made on paper and parchment
carried a meaning. He saw the
soft colours, gold, grey, and silver,
the angles of my body,
the movement of muscle, the
cage that held my heart.
He looked at me and I wondered,
did he see that inside the hare
was a woman's soul?

He painted my eyes, inward
looking, thought-filled. He
painted my ears, listening for
something. He painted my
haunches, strong now, but in my
pose he saw the subtle trust I
placed in him, and perhaps he
did paint the shape of my heart.
I loved him for the way he looked
at me. He gave my wild form the
same honour he would have given
to princes, dukes and saints. He
saw everything that was in me.

And then he took me back to the
fields where I had been found and
he set me free, to live again, to run.

So now, as I sit seeming to be
dreaming in this warm spring
sunlight, I know that the end of
my life is almost come, and when
it does my soul will fly to his
painting, and I will live forever
in that place.

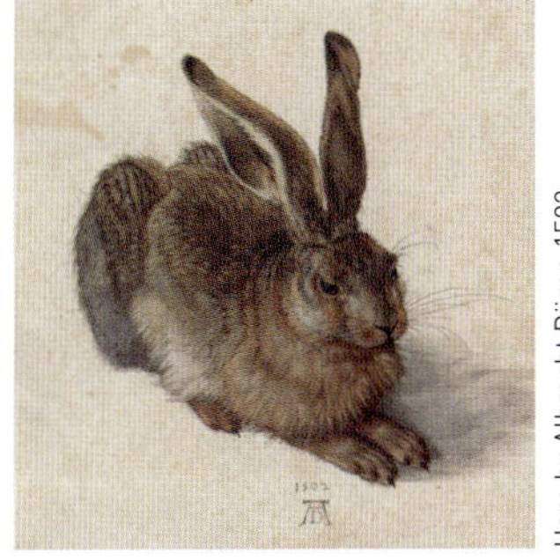

Hare by Albrecht Dürer, 1502

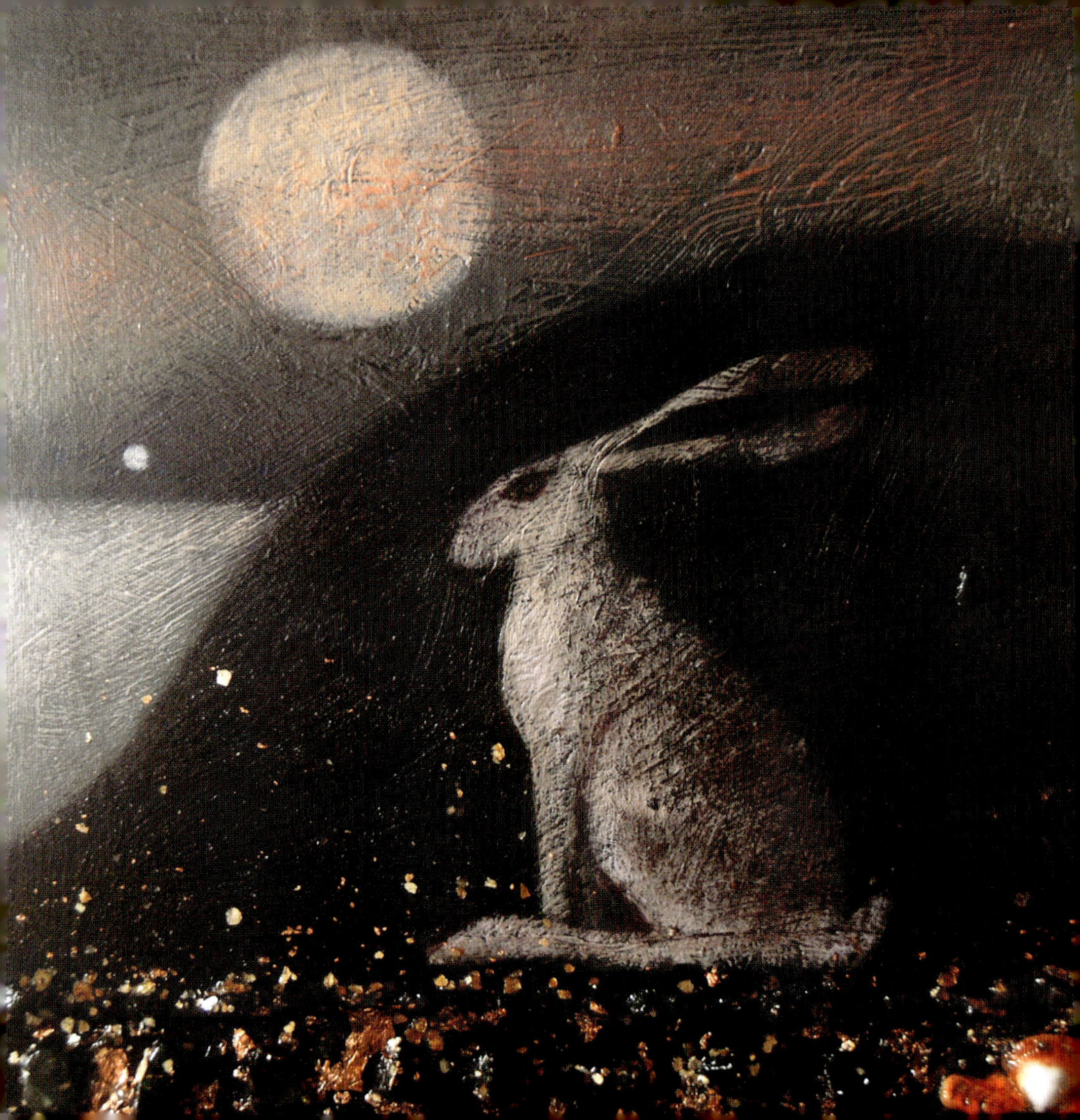

The hare in art and literature

The Decretals of Gregory IX

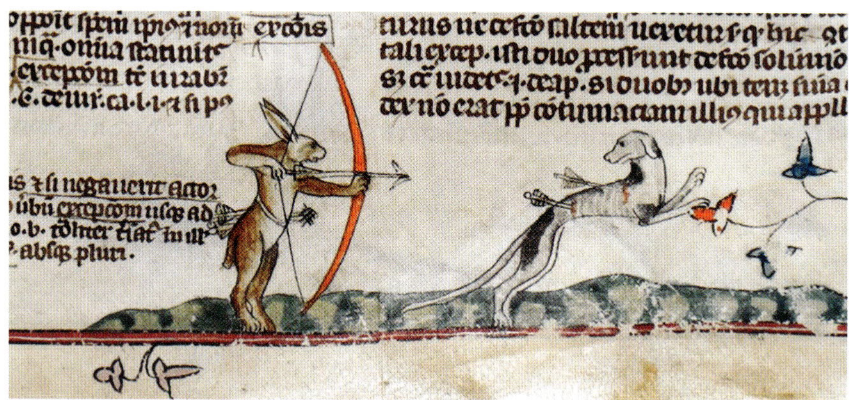

The Decretals of Gregory IX (Latin, Decretales Gregorii IX) are an important source of medieval Canon Law, created in 1230 by St. Raymond of Peñafort for Pope Gregory IX, it is said that it displays the Pope's power over the Universal Church.

This document is of interest to us as hare-lovers because at the bottom of many pages are the most energetic and wicked pen and ink illustrations using a hare to demonstrate a point of law and often showing a reversal of the usual hare and hunter perspective.

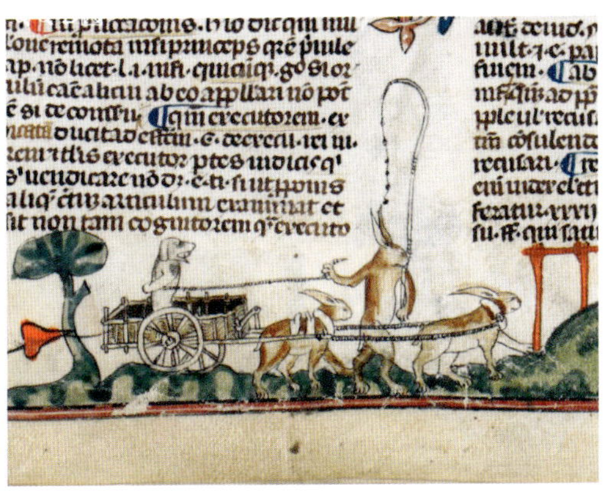

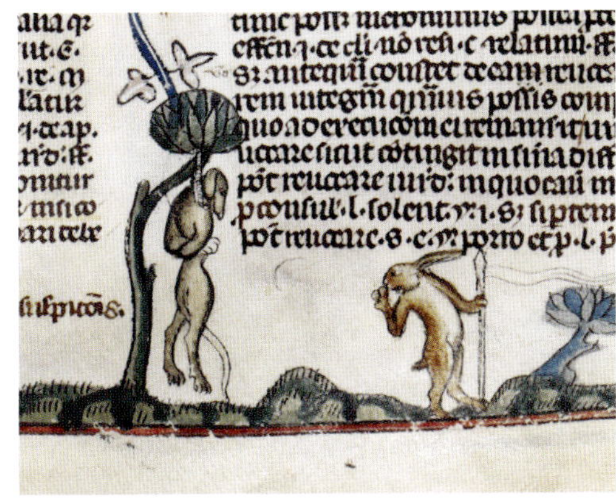

Here the hare is exacting revenge on the lurcher who has chased him hard in the past and on being captured, charged and convicted, the lurcher goes to the gallows in a cart pulled by hares with a hare warder at the cart's side.

Finally the poor dog is strung up and the hare turns back as if to say, 'and let that be a lesson to you'.

William Cowper, the 18th century writer and poet

William Cowper, the 18th century writer and poet, kept three hares as pets in his home in Olney, Buckinghamshire. He and his hares were so well known locally that the town has a weathervane in the market place which commemorates this fact, bearing both a quill pen and... a hare.

He moved to the town in 1768 when he was 37, by which time he had already had some episodes of incapacitating depression and several serious mental breakdowns. The hares originally came into his life to ease these dark dog days and they must have given him some relief as, whilst in Olney, he did some of his best known work, including 'John Gilpin' and the more serious 'The Task'.

We might not have any real detail about his life with his three hares if it were not for a long letter that he wrote about their care to *The Gentleman's Magazine* in 1784. He explained that in 1774 he took in a leveret that had been given to a neighbour's children and was not thriving; he thought that caring for the animal might help his mental state, and so it did. Of course, once he had taken one people offered him more and before he knew it he had three!

'I undertook the care of three, which it is necessary that I should

here distinguish by the names I gave them, Puss, Tiney, and Bess. Notwithstanding the two feminine appellatives, I must inform you that they were all males. I built them houses to sleep in; each had a separate apartment so contrived that their ordure would pass thro' the bottom of it; an earthen pan placed under each received whatsoever fell, which being duly emptied and washed, they were thus kept perfectly sweet and clean. In the daytime they had the range of a hall, and at night retired each to his own bed, never intruding into that of another.'

Cowper explains how they each had their own character. *'Puss was tamed by gentle usage; Tiney was not to be tamed at all: and Bess had a courage and confidence that made him tame from the beginning. I always admitted them into the parlour after supper, when the carpet affording their feet a firm hold, they would frisk and bound and play a thousand gambols, in which, Bess, being remarkably strong and fearless, was always superior to the rest, and proved himself the Vestris of the party (a celebrated French dancer of the day). One evening the cat being in the room had the hardiness to pat Bess upon the cheek, an indignity which he resented by drumming upon her back with such violence, that the cat was happy to escape from under his paws and hide herself.'*

He and his hares were so well known locally that the town has a weathervane bearing both a quill pen and... a hare.

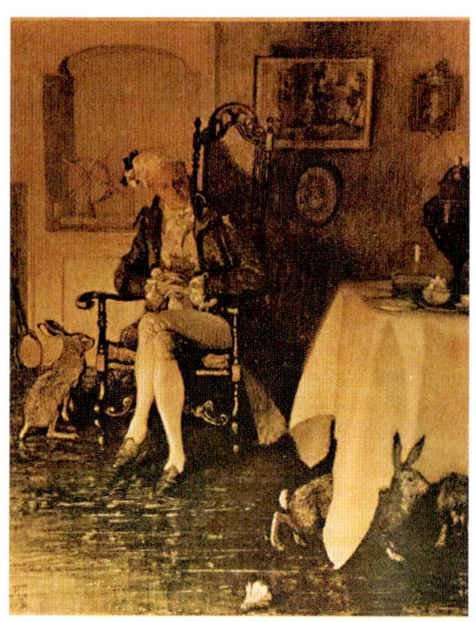

Observing them as he did at such close quarters, he discovered both how curious they were and how discerning in their friendship.

'These creatures have a singular sagacity in discovering the minutest alteration that is made in the place to which they are accustomed, and instantly apply their nose to the examination of a new object. A small hole being burnt in the carpet, it was mended with a patch, and that patch in a moment underwent the strictest scrutiny. They seem too to be very much directed by the smell in the choice of their favourites; so some persons, though they saw them daily, they could never be reconciled, and would even scream when they attempted to touch them; but a miller coming in, engaged their affections at once;

his powdered coat had charms that were irresistible.'

He noted that they liked to eat sand, which he assumed was to aid digestion, loved herbs and had, '*no ill scent belonging to them, that they are indefatigably nice in keeping themselves clean, for which purpose nature has furnished them with a brush under each foot; and that they are never infested by any vermin.'*

Bess died soon after he was full grown but Puss was twelve and Tiney nine when they died, both good ages for a hare and rarely attainable in the wild. Cowper wrote little after the death of Bess but a long eleven verse epitaph for Tiney. It is however on the death of his beloved Puss that we can sense the full poignancy of his love for these wonderful animals.

'*Tuesday, March 9th, 1786. This day died poor Puss, aged eleven years, eleven months. He died between twelve and one at noon, of mere old age, and apparently without pain.'*

He was not a vegetarian and on at least two occasions he obliquely mentioned eating hare. However, throughout his whole life he was a detester of hunting in any shape or form. A supporter of anti-cruelty campaigns, he fought for humanitarian causes and was a staunch opponent of the slave trade.

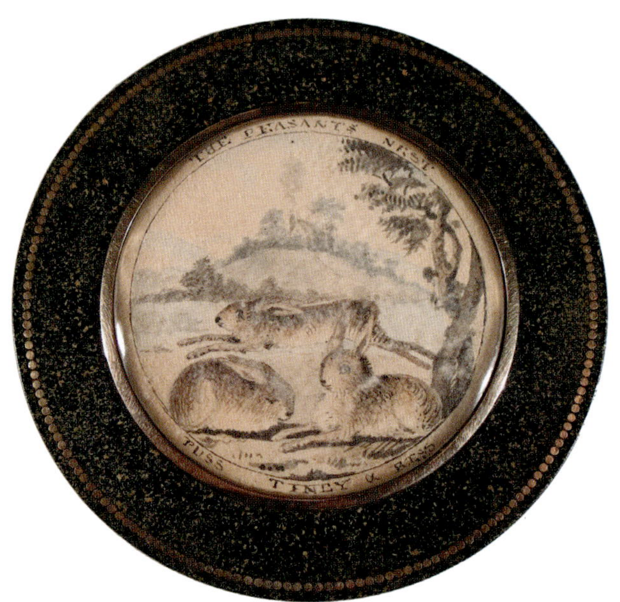

The Cowper and Newton Museum in Olney has much memorabilia concerning Cowper's love of hares and his relationship with Bess, Puss and Tiney.

Cowper's snuff box depicts his three hares, painted by a famous artist of the time 'Romney'. This would have been given to Cowper by his friend William Hayley, who knew 'Romney' as they lived close to each other.

Go to their website, www.cowperandnewtonmuseum.org.uk for details of opening times.

The Story of the Man that went out Shooting

From STRUWWELPETER by Heinrich Hoffman

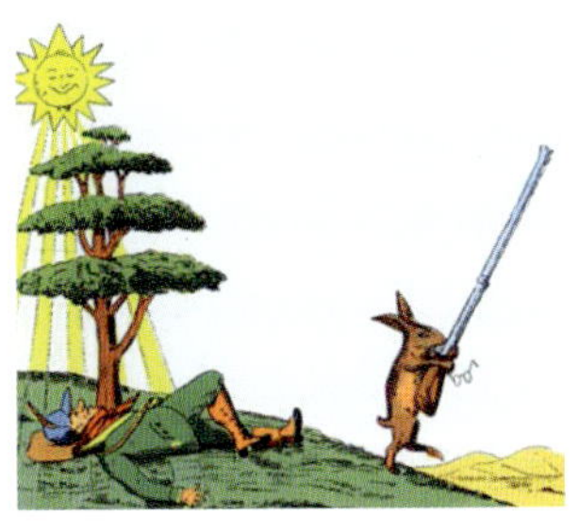

Now, as the sun grew very hot,
And he a heavy gun had got,
He lay down underneath a tree
And went to sleep, as you may see.
And, while he slept like any top,
The little hare came, hop, hop, hop,
Took gun and spectacles, and then
On her hind legs went off again.

The green man wakes and sees her place
The spectacles upon her face;
And now she's trying all she can
To shoot the sleepy, green-coat man.
He cries and screams and runs away;
The hare runs after him all day
And hears him call out everywhere:
"Help! Fire! Help! The Hare! The Hare!"

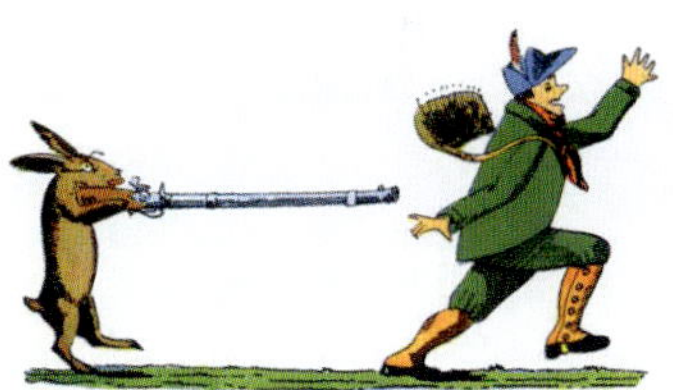

A well-loved Russian folk tale – Grandfather Mazay and the hares

In the 1850s, an old man, Grandfather Mazay (sometimes Mazai), became a legend in his local vicinity for his love and compassion towards the animals, particularly hares, that died annually in the floods around the village where he lived. This area was well known for its floods and, to this end, all the village houses were built on stilts. These were serious floods!

The famous Russian writer and poet Nikolay Nekrasov, who was a friend of Mazay's, was so impressed by his efforts, that in 1870 he wrote a poem about it and by doing so made Mazay's name famous throughout Russia. The poem is called *Grandfather Mazay and the Hares* (Дедушка Мазай и зайцы) and it is now in the Year 3 curriculum in Russian schools.

Grandfather Mazay is telling the story.

'It almost makes me cry, I feel so sorry for the hares when the spring floods arrive. Men run after them and catch them, drown them or beat them to death with sticks. They have no conscience these men.

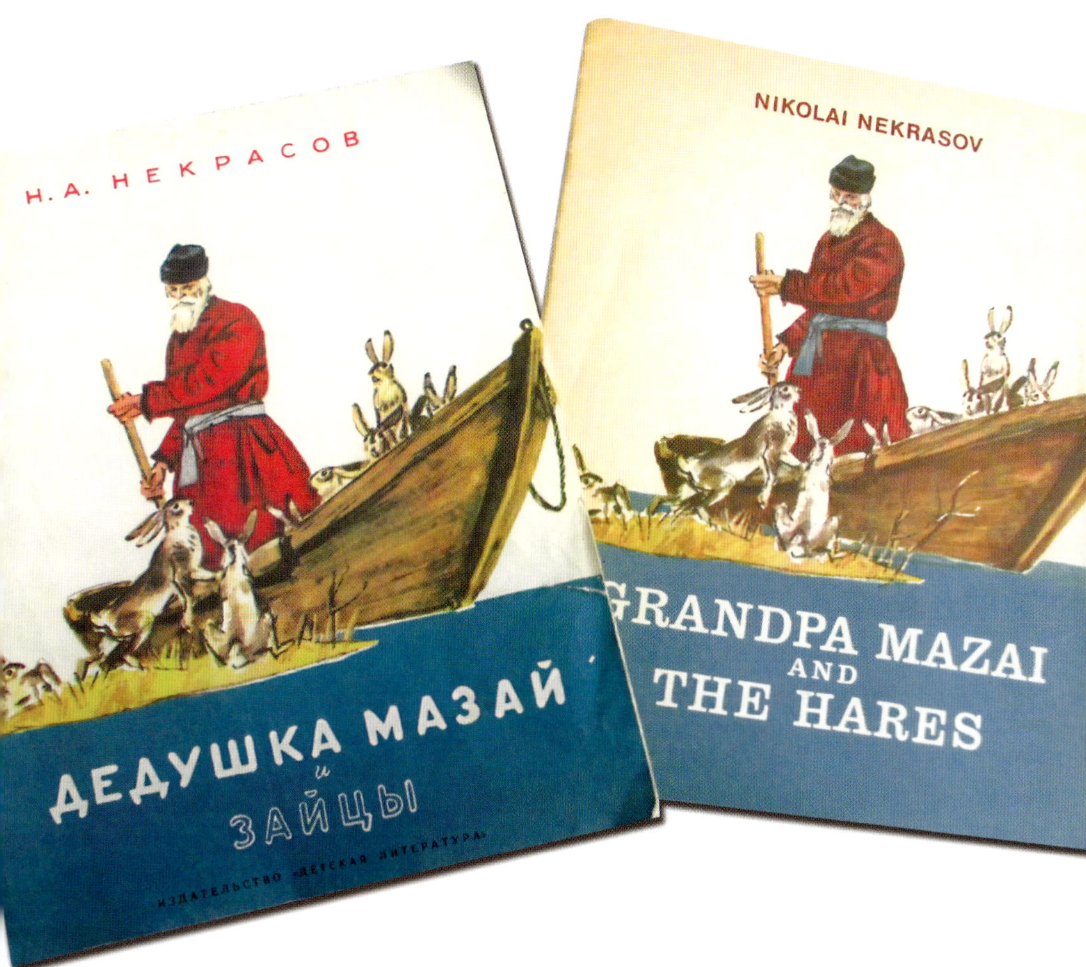

Н. А. НЕКРАСОВ
ДЕДУШКА МАЗАЙ и ЗАЙЦЫ
ИЗДАТЕЛЬСТВО «ДЕТСКАЯ ЛИТЕРАТУРА»
NIKOLAI NEKRASOV
GRANDPA MAZAI AND THE HARES

'One day I went looking for firewood in a boat; there were lots of hares in the water and I started picking them up, when suddenly, I saw a small island full of hares and the water was rising very fast.

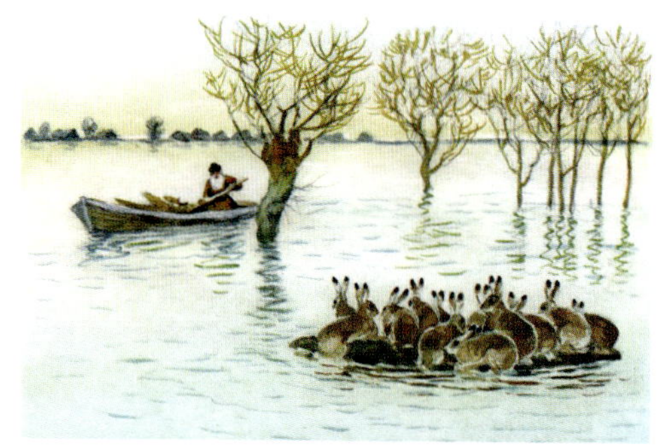

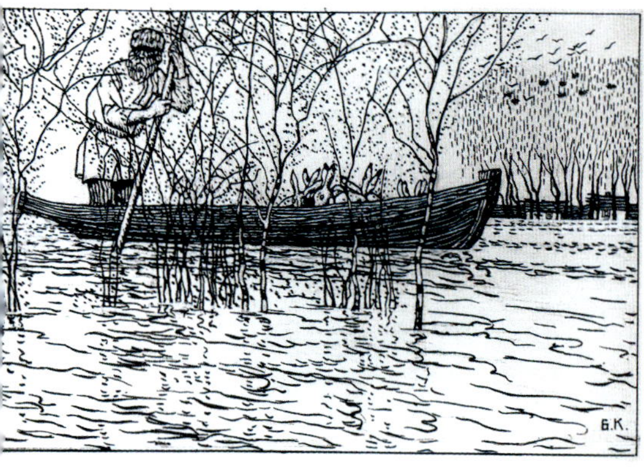

The original ink drawing is kept in the Museum of the Institute of Russian Literature of the Russian Academy of Sciences in St Petersburg.

'I pulled up beside the island and invited them on board but they all held back, until I took one by it's long ears and lifted it in beside me, and then the others, how they jumped! The island quickly disappeared under the water. "You should listen, you hares, to your Grandpa Mazay!" I said.

'Next, I picked up a thin hare standing on a tree stump, followed by a heavily pregnant

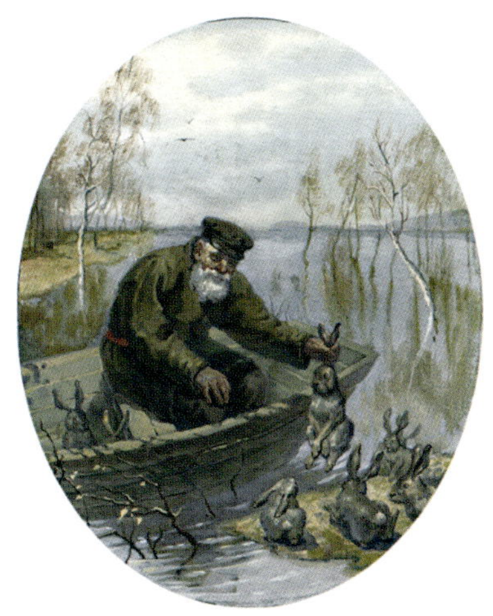

female hare, that I laid in the boat under my coat as she was shivering and barely alive. A log floated by the boat with about a dozen hares on it. "I'd like to take you all but you would sink the boat," I told them but I felt so sorry for them all, I grabbed a knot in the log and towed them behind the boat.

'I caused much hilarity in the village with my 'crew' as we sailed past the village, everyone was laughing. I told them not to disturb my rescue mission. Eventually, we came in sight of a riverbank and all the hares grew excited and started to jostle and rocked the boat and almost stopped me from paddling. I pulled the boat and the log close to the bank and they all made a rush for dry land. "God bless you all," I said as they left, "and don't let me find you in the winter when I'm hunting!"

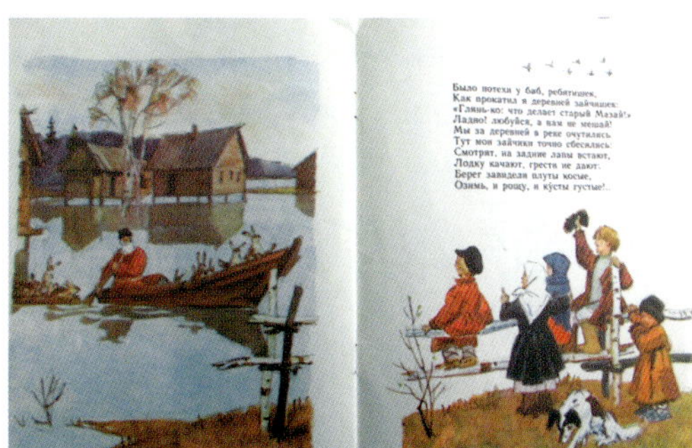

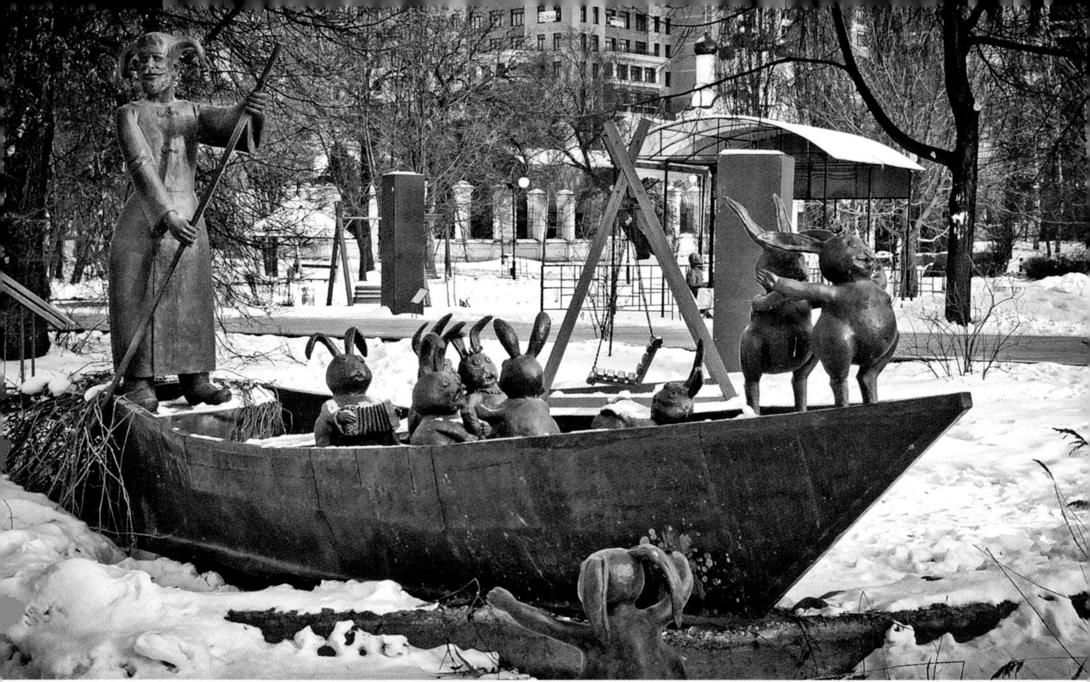

'There were only a couple of hares left in the boat, too wet and weak to run away, so I put them in a sack and took them home, and let them rest in the warmth and fed them and released them the next day, with the same warning – to avoid me at all costs in the winter hunting season.'

This story of the kind-hearted Grandfather Mazay has been depicted many times over the years; for example, a small lacquer box and a big sculpture by Sergey Shilov from Moscow Muzeon Park.

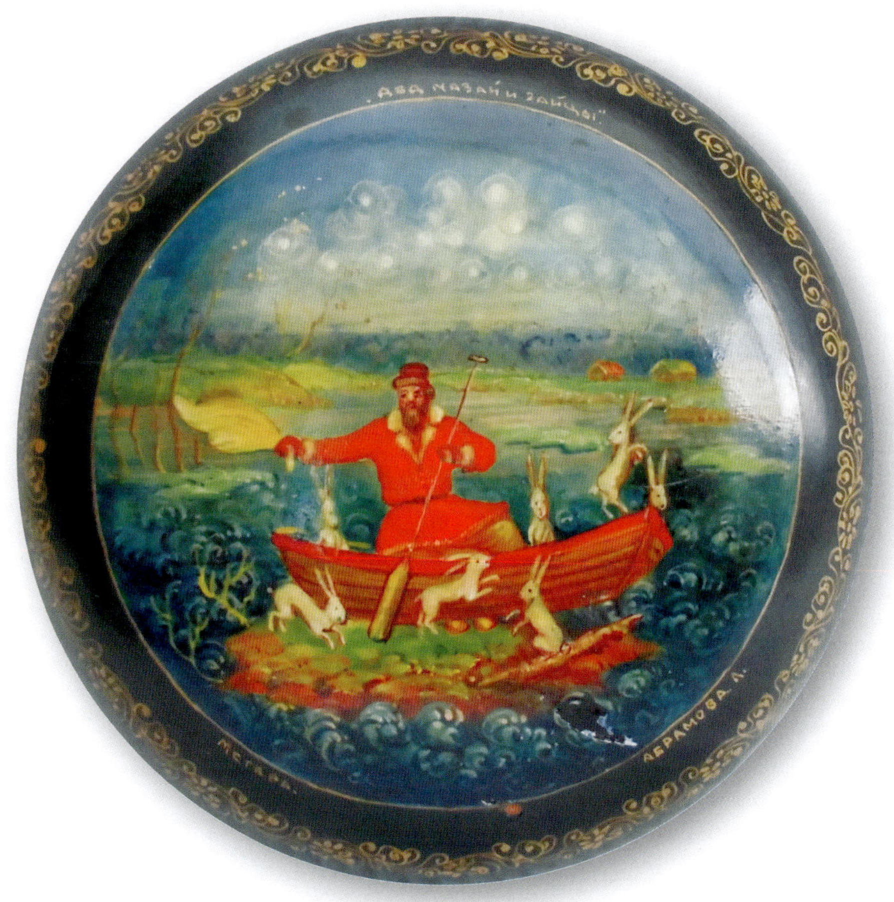

"ДВА МАЗАЙ И ЗАЙЦЫ"
АБРАМОВА Л.

Sir Henry Thornhill collection

Sir Henry Thornhill's love of his grandchildren led him to create the world's largest collection of illustrated correspondence – an amazing 1200+ drawings, postcards and stories.

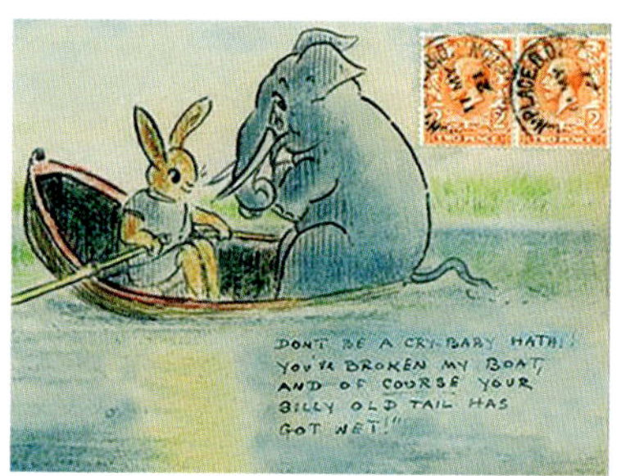

The time was 1914 and Sir Henry was a soldier and administrator for the British Raj in India. He knew his grandchild back in England would grow up without knowing him if he didn't make a special effort to keep communications flowing so he decided to send illustrated picture postcards to his grandson Teddy. (Later Teddy was joined by Margaret, Elizabeth and Anne.) The cards covered all aspects of nature in India. He also told tales of Hathi the elephant and his friend Mr. Hare who had many adventures.

He never, poor man, had the chance to actually be with his beloved grandchildren because on his return to England the family was posted to India!

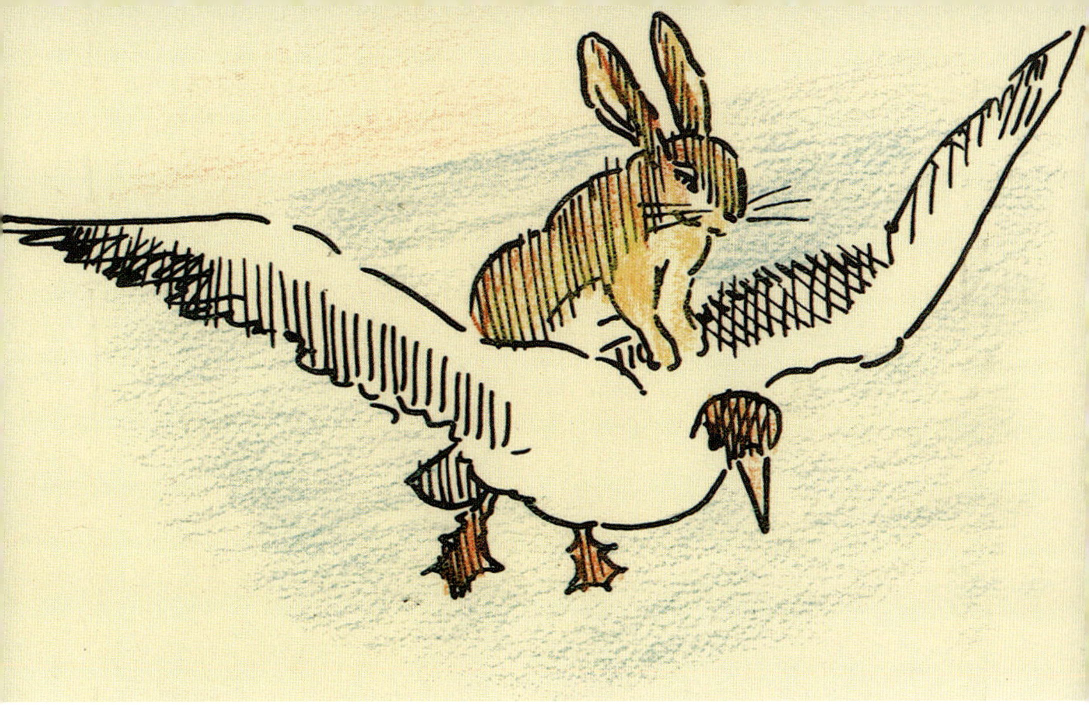

However, he continued to write
to them all every week for the
next 15 years. Needless to say, all
the letters and cards were kept,
and they lay undisturbed until
rediscovered in the 1970s.
There is a wonderful website,
www.ultimategrandparent.com
where you can hear the stories
read by his great-grandson and
see the illustrations. There is
a lovely book too, *Pictures in
the Post: the Illustrated Letters
of Sir Henry Thornhill to His
Grandchildren* edited by
Michael Baker.

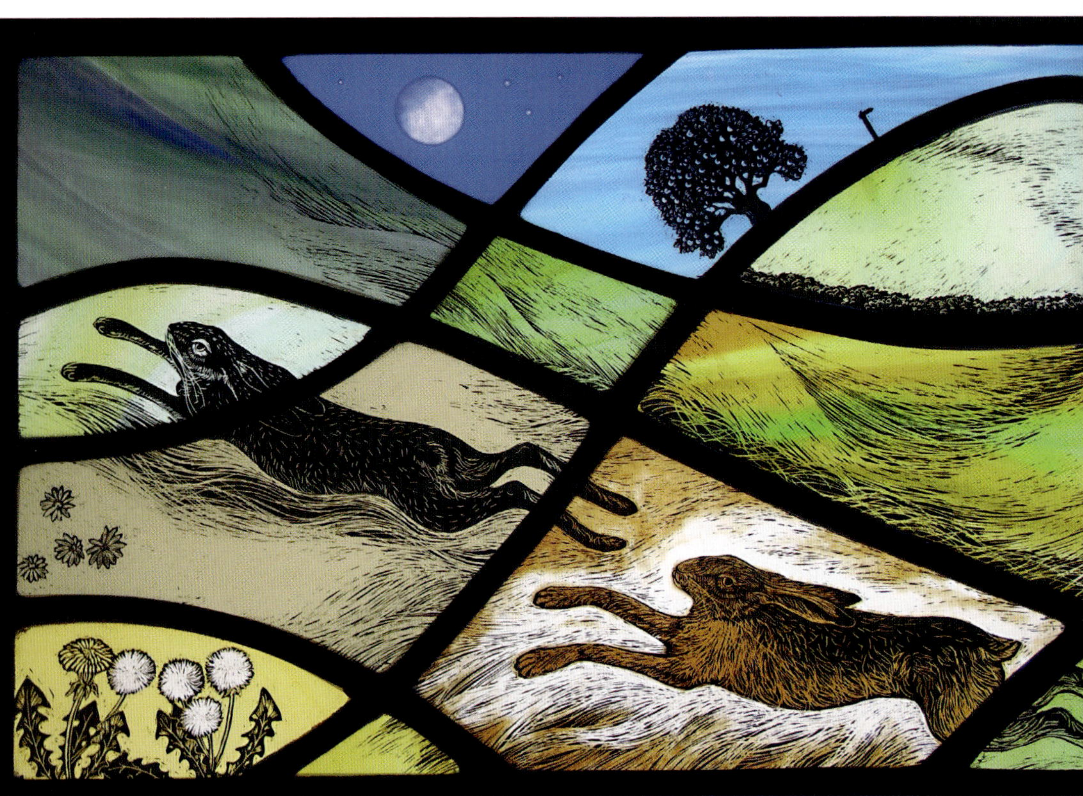

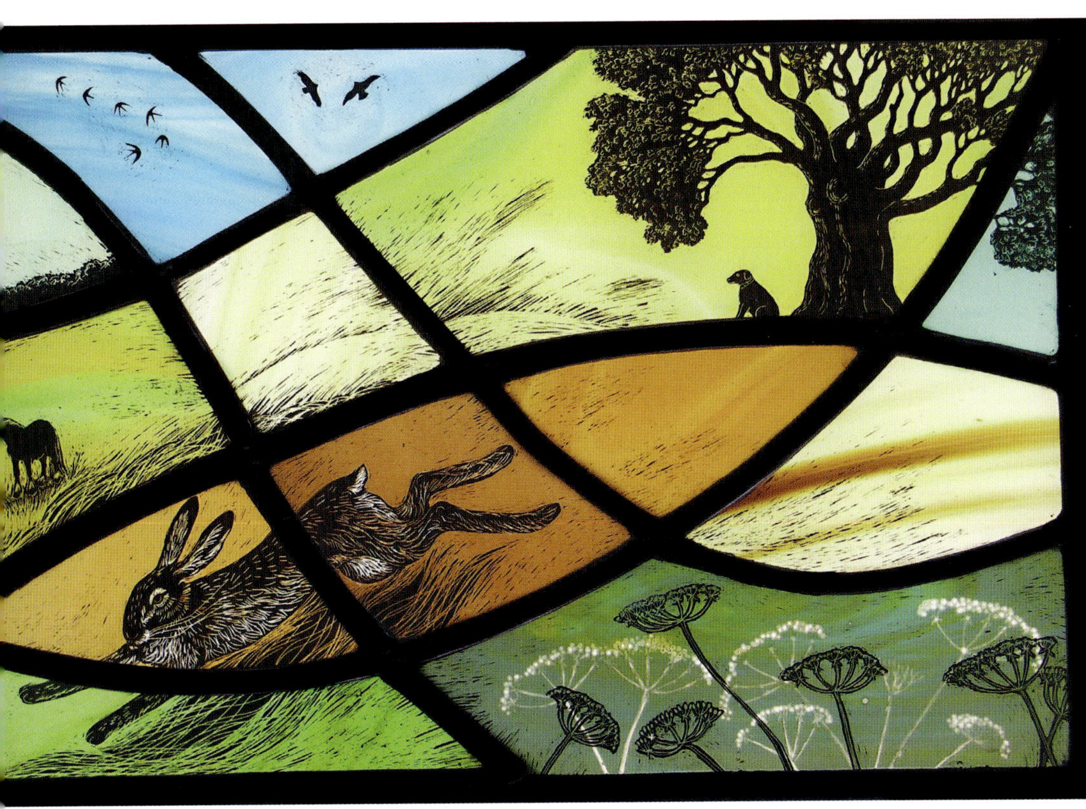

A Brown Hare

I saw a lone Brown Hare
One of the wild unshod
Whose fleet feet kiss the sods
Runner for the joy of it
Patter cake boxer
Muse for myriad artworks
Its ink dipped charcoal tipped ears
Gave me the ancient archers' salute
It amber eyed me with a look I read as pity
For me whose toes will never melt
The icing sugar early frost
Or crackle summer stubble
Always a barrier between
My sole and fecund earth
I hope your genes run on forever
I'll watch for them in Porlock Vale
Or Dunkery Hill
When it's cold enough
To see a hare's breath

Stephen Lewis HPT member April 2014
Included in 'MIDNIGHT SKIES Exmoor in verse'

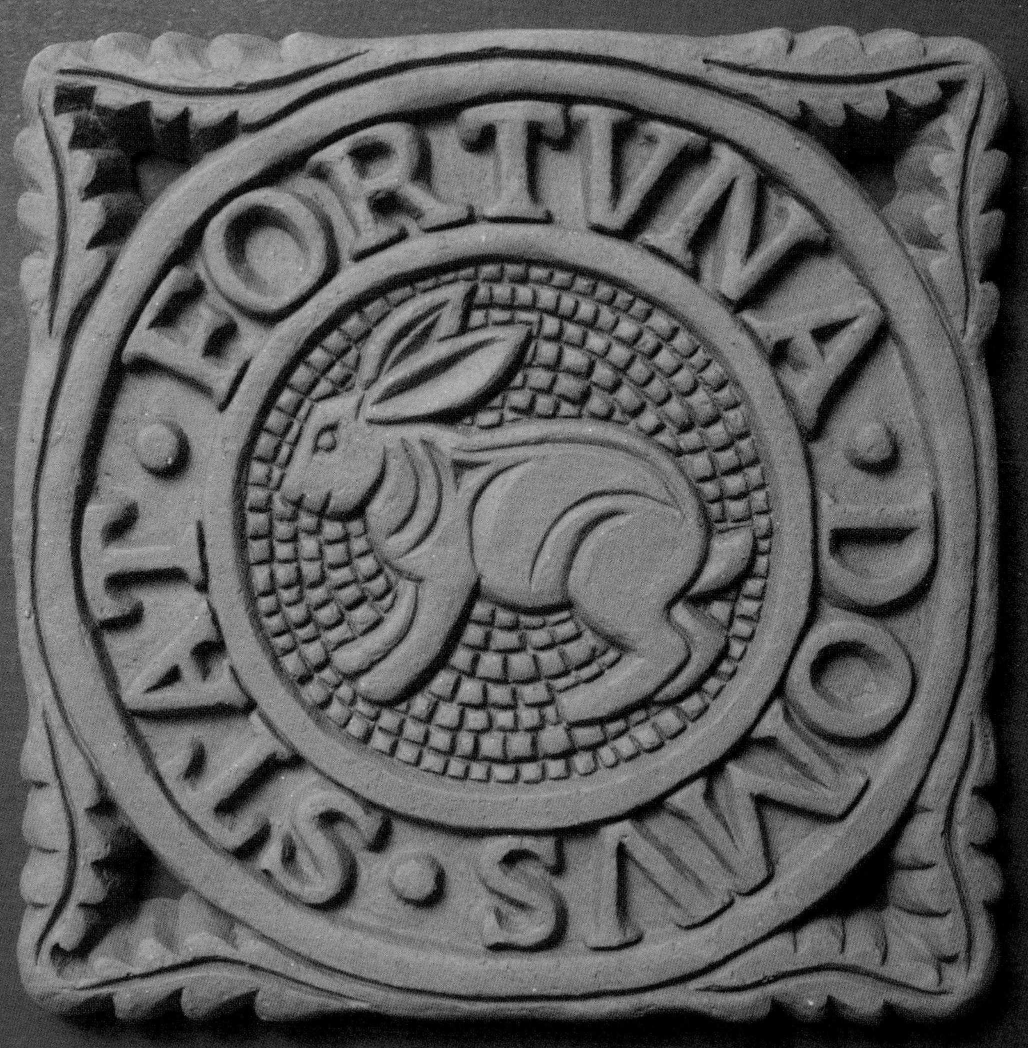

FORTVNA · DOMVS · STVLTIS · FORTVNA

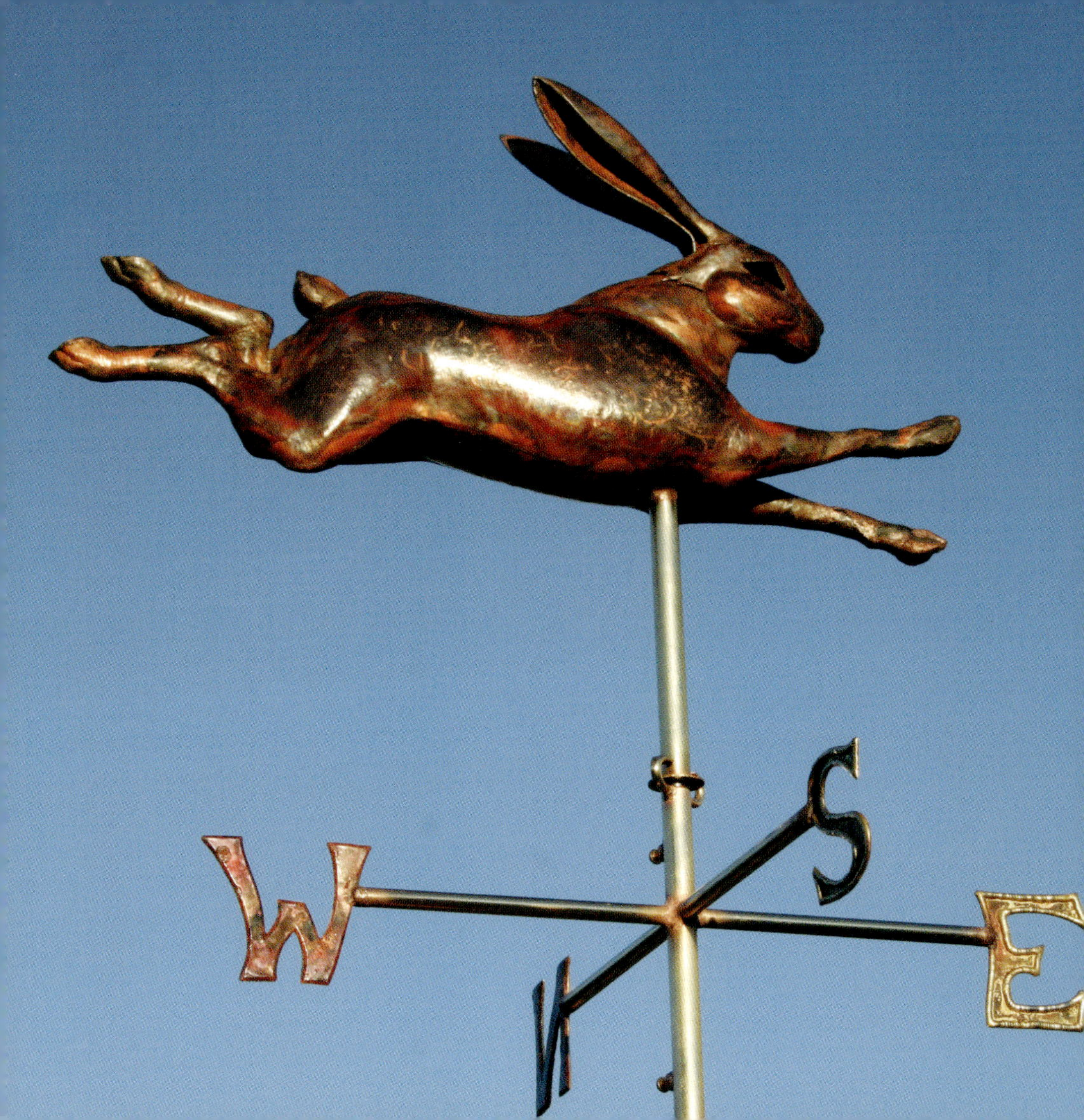

Dream

For FlR

A long lost legionary's living larder,
a courser's cold-eyed calculation,
a sleek greyhound's golden goal,
a pre-modern cuisine classic.
Hilarious high-kicking parkland pugilist,
ballsy boxer, amber-eyed seducer,
rapid runner with innate lagomorphic legerdemain,
a complement to the countryside,
a beautiful brown hare.

Charles Middleburgh

Hare Piece

Crows are conjuring the dusk.
The moon's a bitten bit of rusk.

Buzzard sings her mewing cry,
Prowling, feathered cat-of-sky

And there among the winter beet
I'm given grace, a priceless treat

For tired, telescopic eyes:
Two hares, and then to my surprise

They stand, each balanced like a boy
Their stance a circus trick of joy.

They push out paws, begin to fight,
A furry flash of grey and white,

Such a bold and brave display
As on hind legs they swerve and
sway,

Ears stuck up like lollipops,
I breathe too loud, the battle stops.

They turn to statues cut from bark.
I blink. They sprint into the dark,

Leaving me to simply stare
At a dream no longer there.

Oh what delights this world unlocks
To let me see two hares that box.

Andrew Fusek Peters

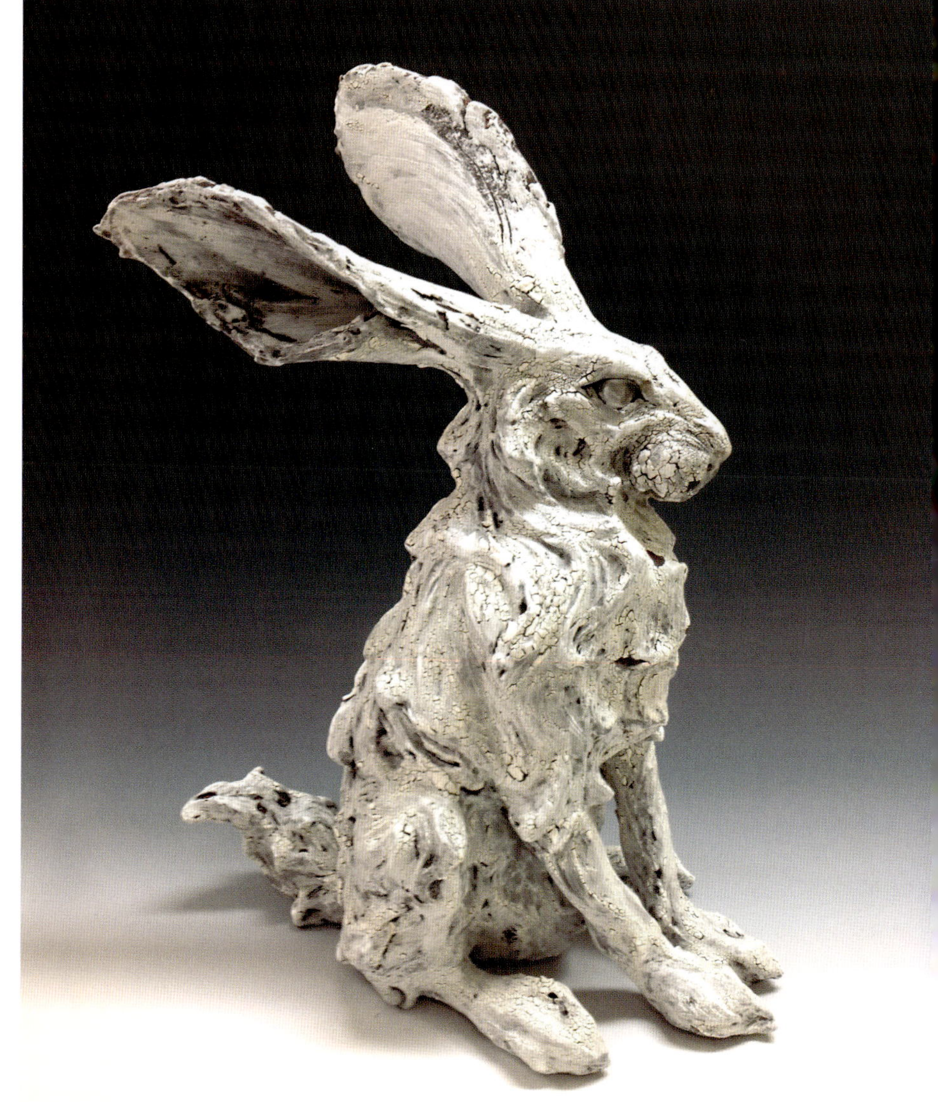

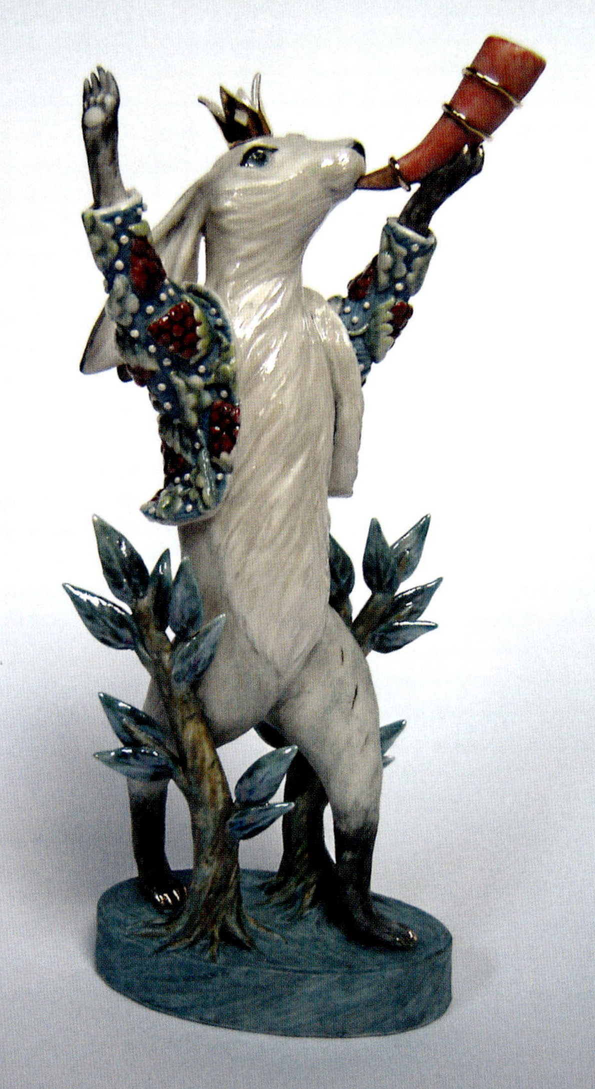

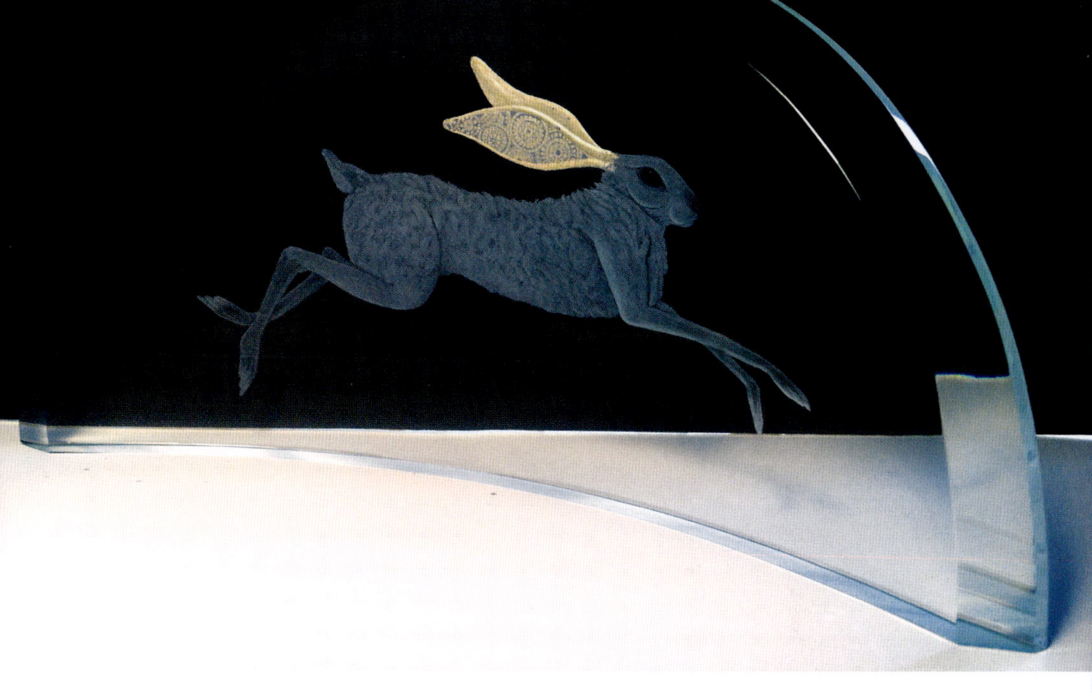

Ballad of Running Hare!

she runs to save her life from all that would be cruel!
she runs to stop her life being over far too soon!
born into a world where there is no redress!
born into the field where beasts set her tests!
she submits to the order around!

she runs to take cover and lead them astray!
she runs to seek help from those who betray!
born into a world are her leverets bright!
born into danger where dark stalks with light!
they submit to the order around!

her expectations take on mortal fear!
her eyes and her ears ever wary and keen!
her stillness belies the intense need to rear!
yet another small group of the vulnerable pups!
she submits to the order around!

her mate is as keen to keep hopes alive!
he runs and protects them so dies as he tries!
the babies stay living for just one more day!
both mother and father died in the affray!
they submit to the order today!

Denny Bradbury

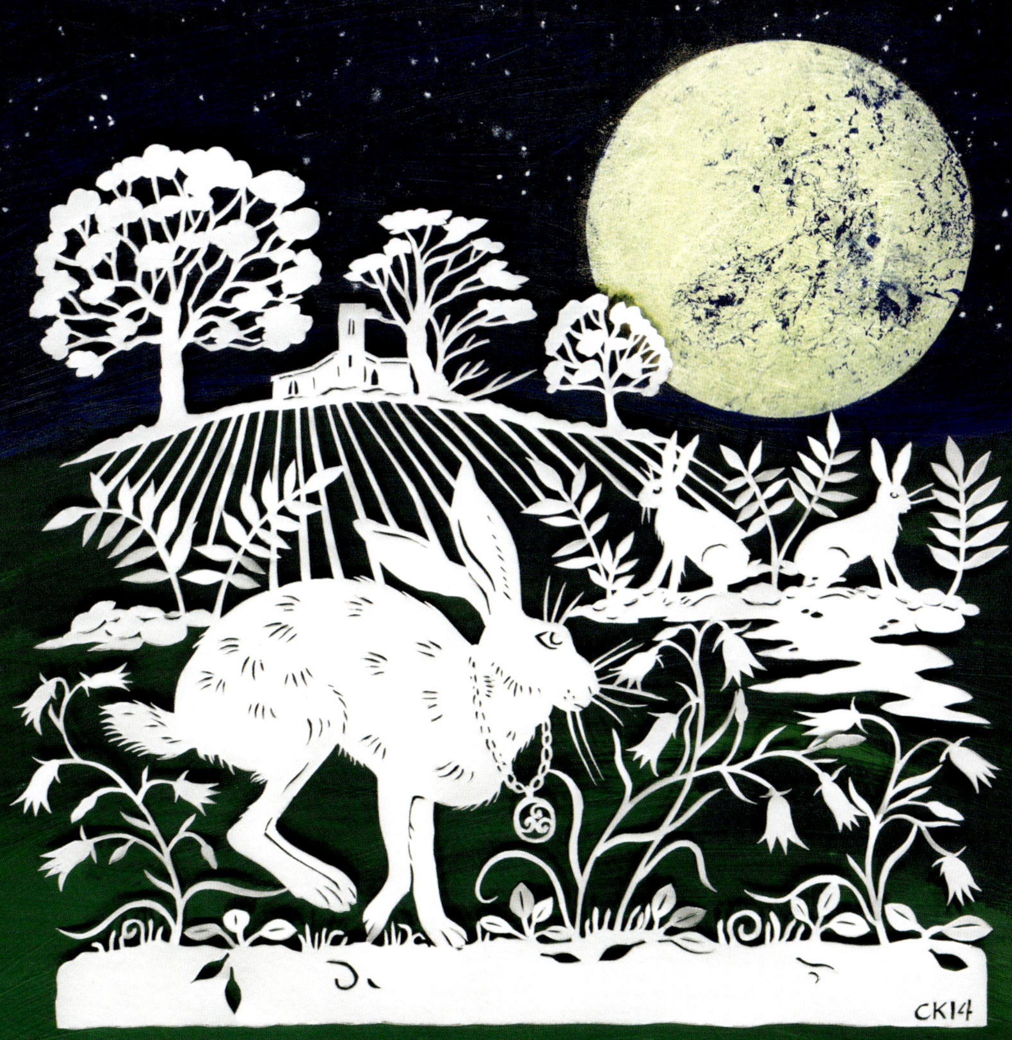
CK14

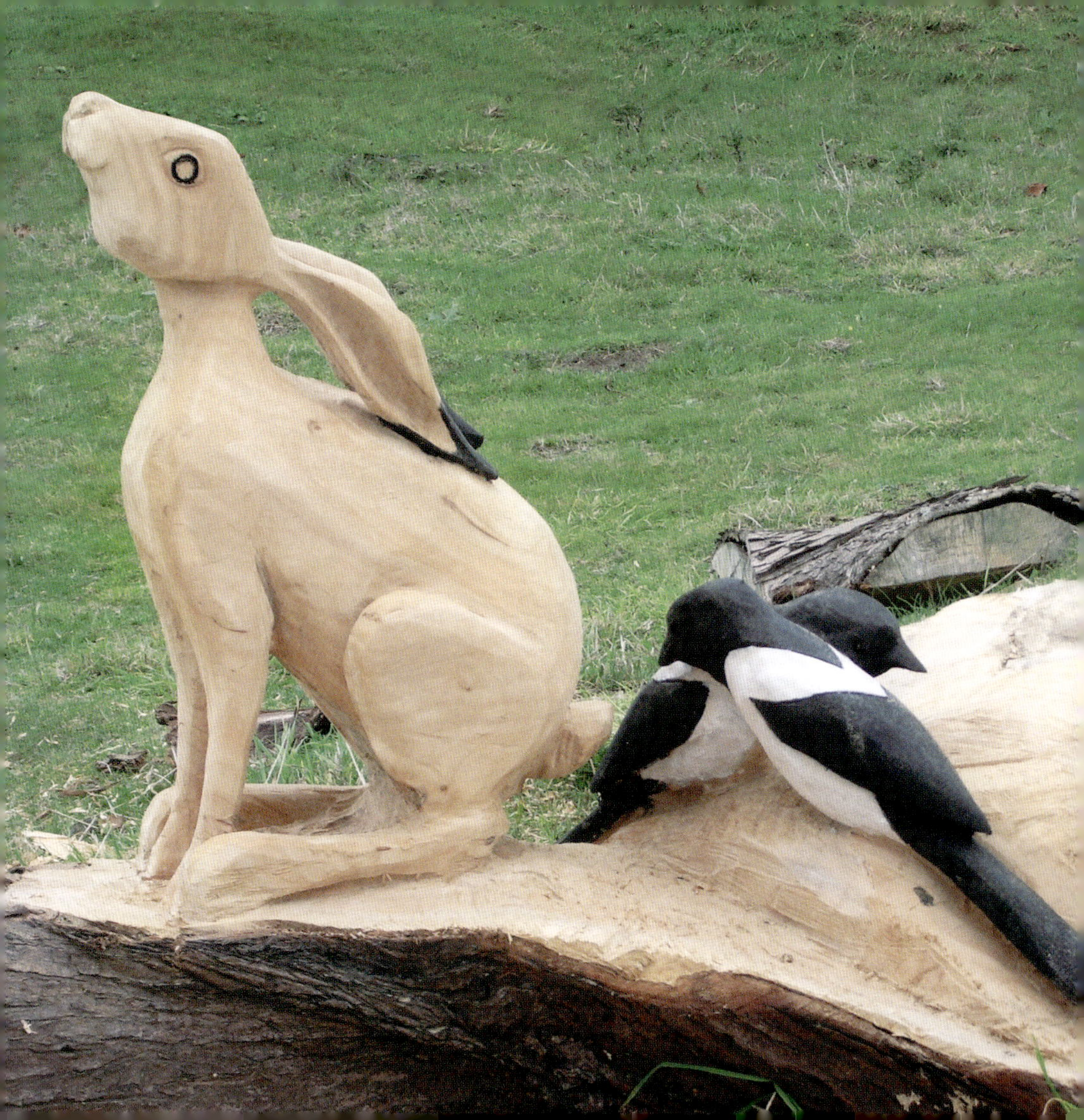

Hare

A quietness now,
Scratched by the pen of crow
On crumpled sky.

Pigeons flare,
Unfurling a shock
Of feathers,
Flags of the wind.

Hare is near,
Ears pricking at the February mist
Like forks,
Tuned to all approach.

One breath too loud,
And hare's legs pitch
In a leopard dreaming.
One sprint
And he is gone,
Swallowed by the cold tongue of twilight.

Andrew Fusek Peters

The Hare

Poised in the furrow
Of a ploughed field
A hare quivers
Expectantly,
Sniffing the air,
Intoxicated
With new life
Its paws box the air
Exultantly.

Sue Mackrell

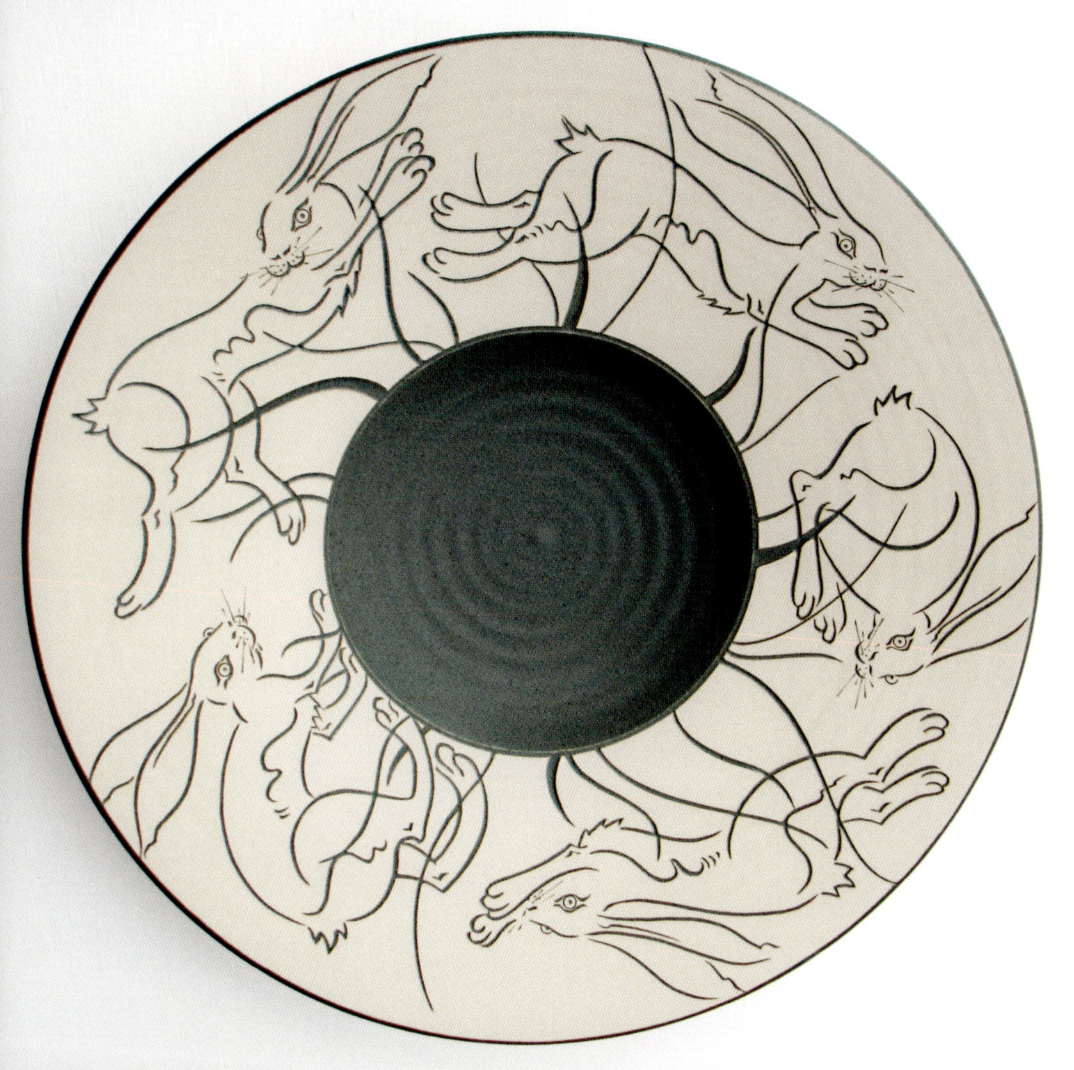

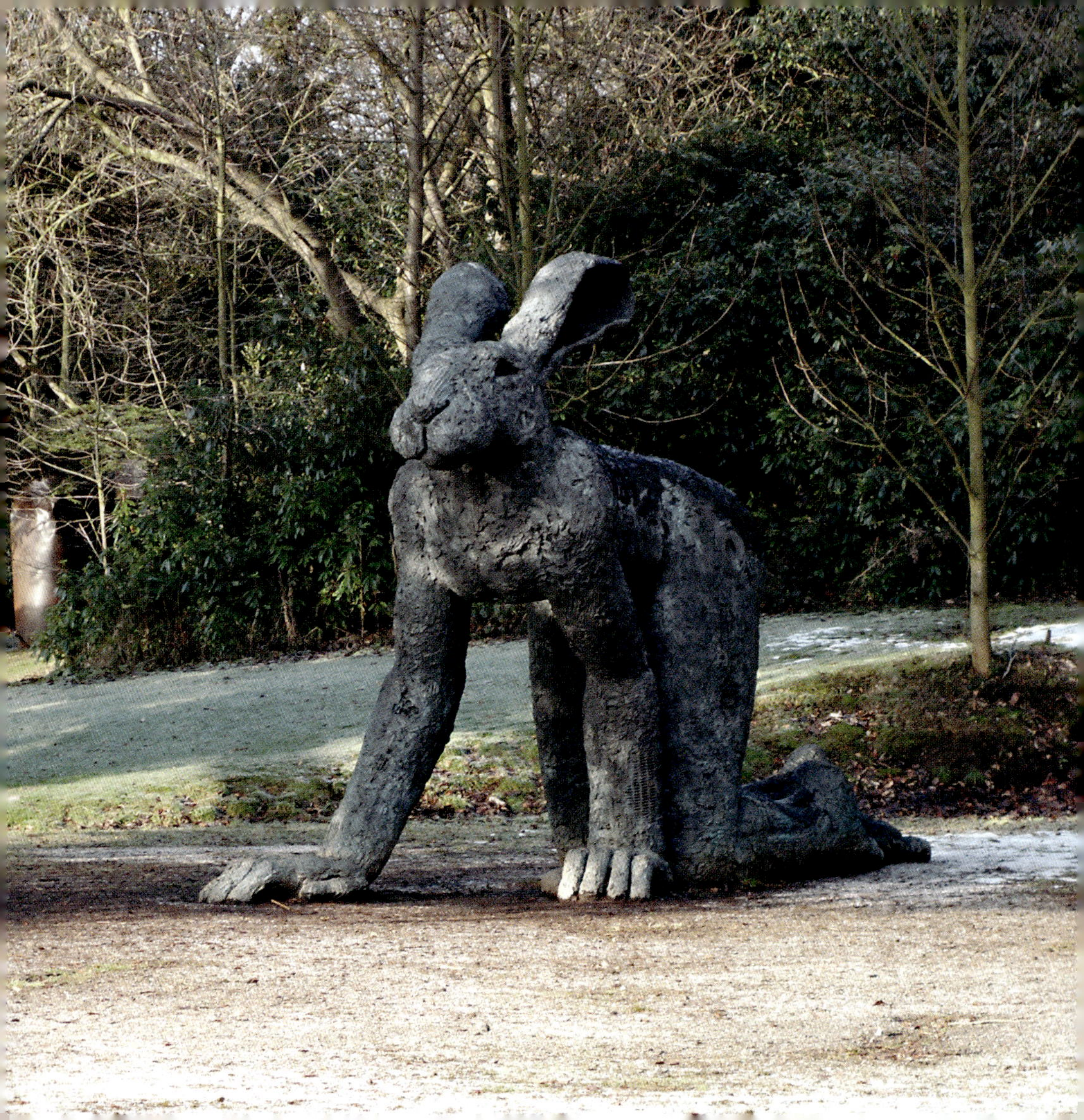

Hare today

Hare today Hare tomorrow
Hare forlorn
There's a need
Of time to borrow
Shooting us
Is simply greed
Why the fuss
We'll never know
Nibbling corn
Just makes it grow.

Mal Jones
Member, regular correspondent and birdwatcher.

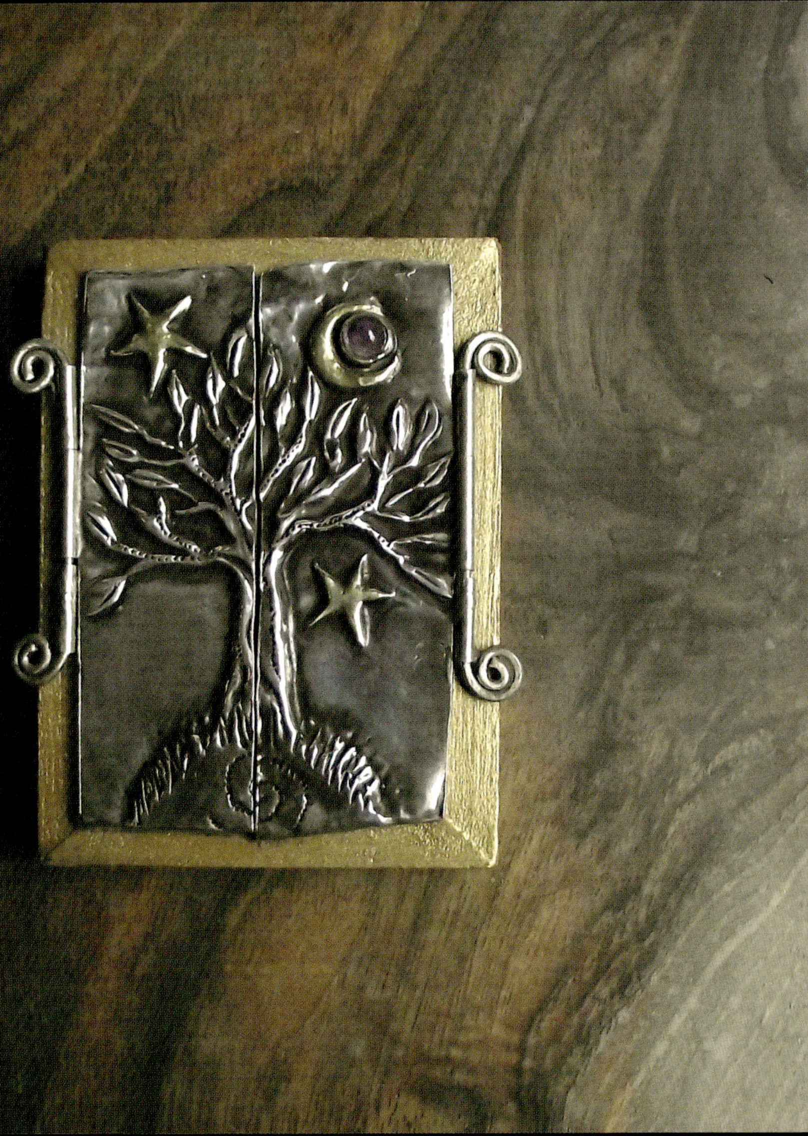

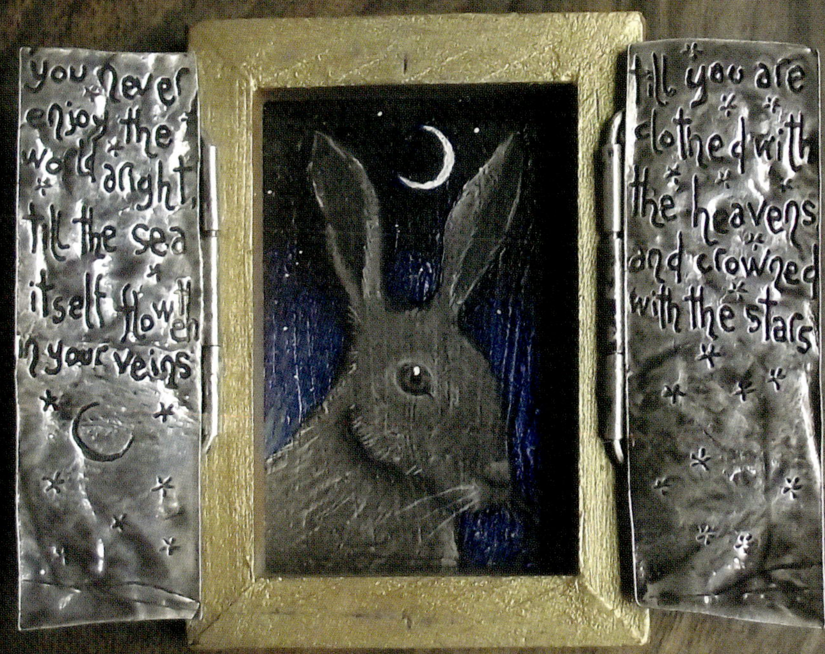
you never enjoy the world aright, till the sea itself floweth in your veins
till you are clothed with the heavens and crowned with the stars

Artworks

Page 101: St Anselm by Mick Toole

Page 114 and 118: The Old Hare in Spring: 1502 by Jackie Morris
www.jackiemorris.co.uk

Page 120: At the Edge of the Silver Sea by Catherine Hyde
www.catherinehyde.co.uk

Page 138/139: Hares a'running by Tamsin Abbott
Tamsin Abbott, Bishops Frome, Herefordshire
Tel 01531 640005

Page 141: STAT FORTUNA DOMUS by Black Dog of Wells
www.blackdogofwells.com
This hare is based on a mosaic found by archaeologists in the floor of a Romano-Celtic villa in Cirencester. Inscribed into the tile are the words, attributed to the classical poet Virgil, 'Stat Fortuna Domus' which can be translated as 'Good Fortune to this House'.

Page 142: Hollow-bodied Hare Weathervane
Hollow-bodied Hare Weathervane Copper, brass & bronze. 64 cm long
Greens Weathervanes (2014)
www.greensvanes.co.uk

Page 145: Winter hare by Mary Philpott
Mary Philpott is a ceramicist from Ontario, Canada. 101 Shakespeare Street. Stratford ON Canada N5A3W5
www.VerdantTileCo.com

Page 146: Hare and Horn by Eleanor Bartleman
www.eleanorbartleman.co.uk

Page 147: Golden eared hare by Nancy Sutcliffe
www.nancysutcliffe.co.uk
nancy@nancysutcliffe.co.uk
www.facebook.com/NancySutcliffeGlassEngraver

Page 149: Paper Cut Artwork by Claire Knight.
info@hareandmoongallery.co.uk

Page 150: The Good Omen by Paul Sivell
The Good Omen, which stands at a cross roads on the Isle of White, carved from a fallen Leyland Cypress it was commissioned by Arreton Parish Council. www.thecarvedtree.com.

Page 153: Incised hare plate by Louise Darby
Louise Darby
Clay Barn, Redhill, Alcester, Warwickshire B49 6NQ
Tel 01789 765214
louisedarby@louisedarby.co.uk

Page 154: Crawling Lady Hare at the Yorkshire Sculpture Park by Sophie Ryder
www.sophie-ryder.com

Page 156/157: Hare Icon by Hannah Willow
www.hannah.willow.com
www.facebook.com/Hannah.willow.artist
Email willowhannah@gmail.com

End paper and Hare Encounters linocuts from "Why a Hare is Not a Rabbit" by Jane Russ.

Photography

Sue Alderman, pages 13, 31 top right, 64, back cover 2nd from left.

Ben Andrew, page 63.

Maggie Bruce, page 62.

Nick Burton, page 24.

Jon Evans, pages 4, 42, 44, 90, back cover 3rd from left.

Andrew Fusek Peters, front cover and pages 25, 72.

Sarah Hanson, page 10.

Andrew Howard, pages 23, 28, 29.

Andrew Kelly, pages 48, 50, 51, 53, 54, 56.

Catriona Komlosi, pages 26, 31 bottom right, 32, 40, 46-47.

Franz Komlosi, pages 31 top left, 34-35, 37, 38-39.

Terry Larwood, page 8.

Robert McEwen, pages 22, 31 bottom left, 43, 60-61, back cover 4th from left.

Russ Miles, pages 7, 14, 16-17, 58, 68-69, 75, 76, 78, back cover 1st from left.

Kevin Sawford, page 21.

Andrew Smith, page 70.

John Whyte-Venables, page 18.

Acknowledgments

My gratitude to:

The wonderfully generous writers, photographers and artists who have let me use their work free of charge and helped make this book such a thing of beauty.

The Committee of the HPT, for their continued enthusiasm for this project.

Pip Kay for the images of her Grandfather Masay books and snuff box.

Gilly Middleburgh for her supportive copy editing/proofing "enough with the hares" Mrs. M but I did finish it in the end!

Finally very big thanks to my husband Mick Toole, who not only had to put up with my wittering about hares non-stop but even pulled a wonderful illustration out of his head and hand, when I couldn't find what I needed!!

Jane Russ - February 2015

The Hare Book, Hare Preservation Trust
Published in Great Britain in 2014 by
Graffeg Limited.
ISBN 9781909823686

Text by Jane Russ copyright © 2014.
Designed and produced by Graffeg
Limited copyright © 2014.

This edition 2026.

Graffeg Limited, 15 Neptune Court,
Vanguard Way, Cardiff, CF24 5PJ, Wales,
UK. Tel: 01554 824000. croeso@graffeg.
com. www.graffeg.com.

Jane Russ is hereby identified as the
author of this work in accordance with
section 77 of the Copyright, Designs and
Patents Act 1988.

Printed by 1010 Printing, China.

A CIP Catalogue record for this book is
available from the British Library.

This book is designed for general readers,
printed with materials and processes that
are safe and meet all applicable European
safety requirements. The book does not
contain elements that could pose health
or safety risks under normal and intended
use.

We hereby declare that this product
complies with all applicable requirements
of the General Product Safety Regulation
(GPSR) and any other relevant EU
legislation.

Appointed EU Representative:
Easy Access System Europe Oü, 16879218
Mustamäe tee 50, 10621, Tallinn, Estonia
gpsr.requests@easproject.com

The publisher gratefully acknowledges
the financial support of this book
by the Books Council of Wales.
www.gwales.com.

4 5 6 7 8 9

Link to our
Nature Books

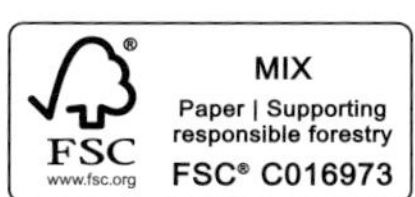

Books in the Nature Series

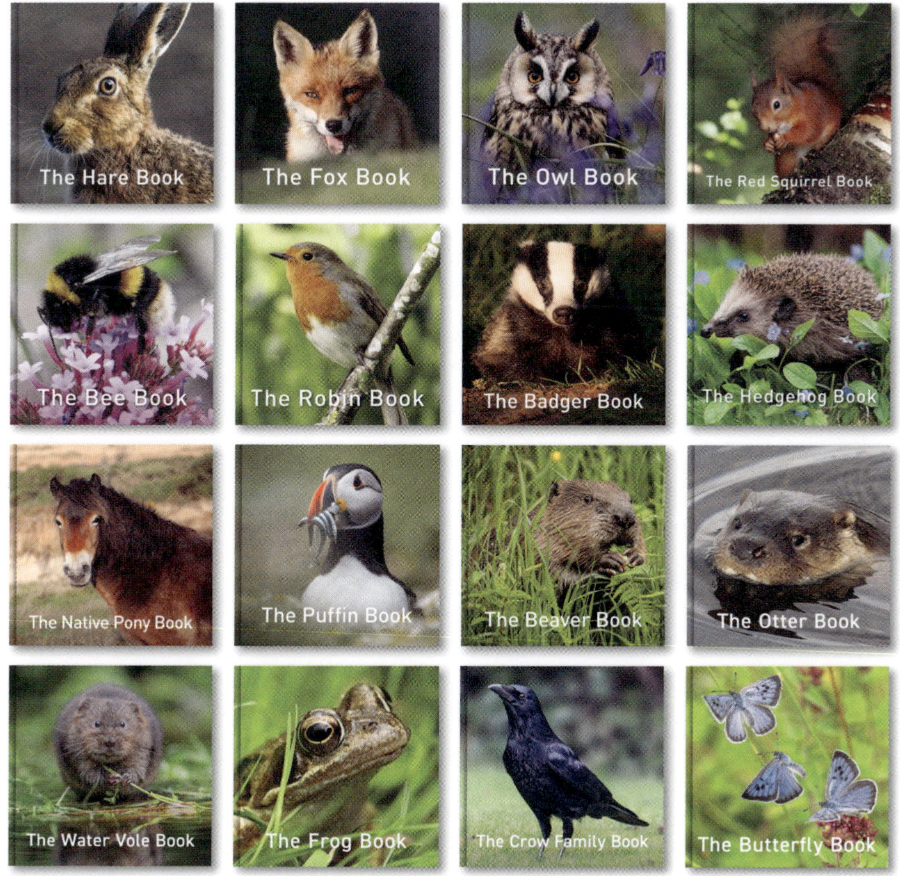

www.graffeg.com

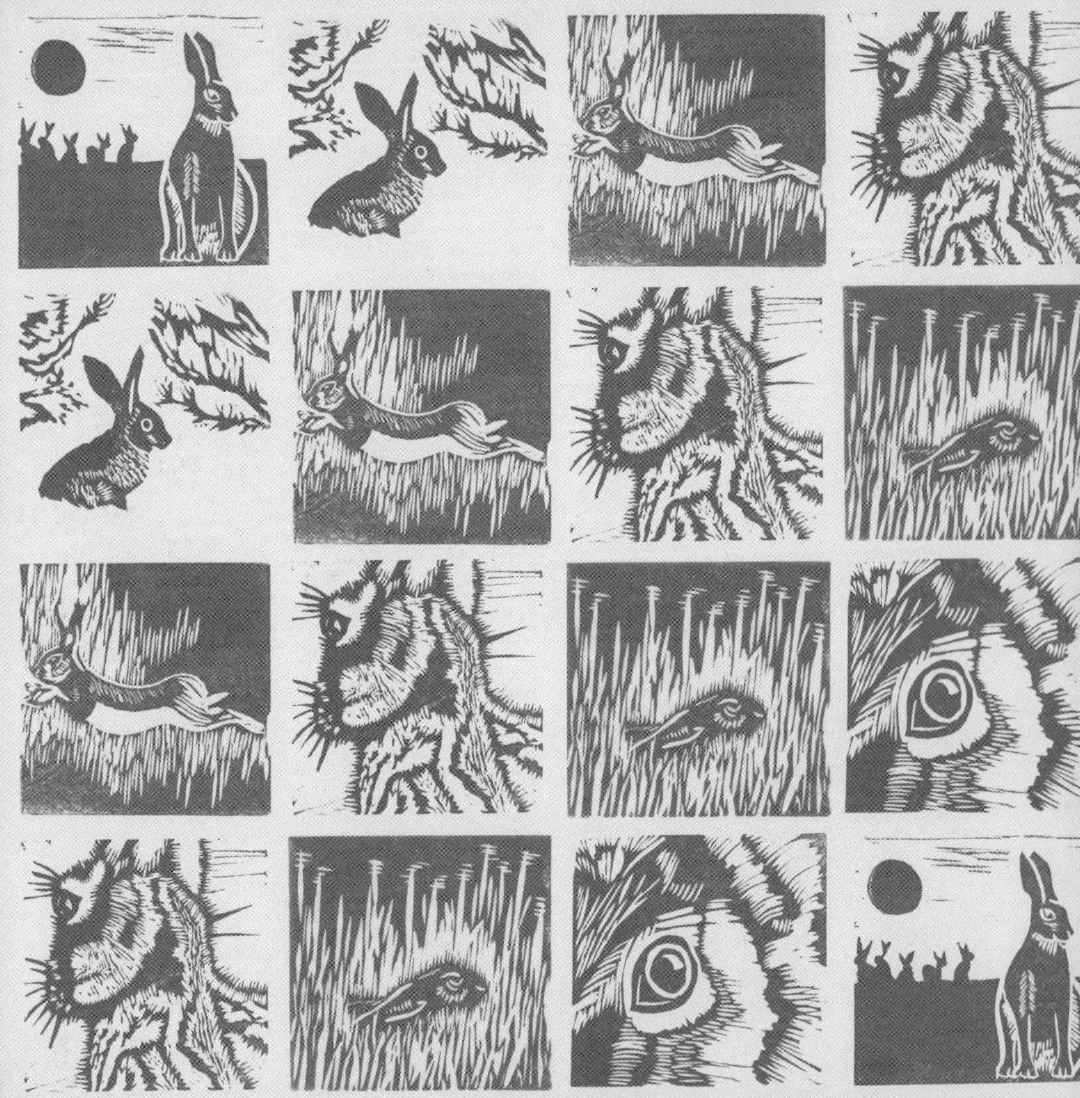